# PREFACE.

—

WHEN Bishop Percy's work, the *Reliques of Ancient English Poetry*, issued from the press, the poetry of our country was in a very weak and languishing condition; for whilst the only poetry read and appreciated by the learned of the day, was that of the philosophic school, the taste of the masses was of a still more debased character, as amongst them nothing was popular but sickly and unnatural pastorals: and thus, between a very questionable philosophy of pantheistic tendency on the one hand, and a mock arcadianism, with its accompaniment of Damons, and Delias, and Strephons, and sheep and brooks and crooks, on the other, nature and truth were lost sight of, and the inspiration of the bard had well nigh become a thing unknown.

Percy's great work (great, notwithstanding all its omissions, its errors, and its imperfections) prepared the way for a better state of things, and brought about a poetical revolution—a new era in our literature, still in progress, and which has been adorned by such names as Goldsmith, Gray, Collins, Cowper, Crabbe, Campbell, Scott, and

Wordsworth. All honour, therefore, to the memory of Bishop Percy! While, however, we honour the reformer, let us never forget the sources of his inspiration, those

> " Sweet poets of the gentle antique line,
> Who made the hue of beauty all eterne,
> And gave earth's melodies a silver turn,"

nor, that one of such minstrel bards was Thomas Deloney of Norwich, the author of " that little ancient miscellany entitled The Garland of Good-Will". Of the biography of Thomas Deloney, or Delone, (for we have the name in both forms) little is known beyond the few facts collected by Mr. Collier; it would appear that the minstrel was a silk weaver, who made his poetical *debút* at Norwich, about the year 1586, and who continued to write and amuse the public until near the time of his decease, which occurred in 1600. Our author evidently enjoyed no small share of popularity, and to which his merits well entitled him; nor was his fame confined to his own order, for even the elegant and classic Drayton, in an allusion to his " rhyme," designates it " full of state and pleasing." Deloney was unquestionably a man of talent, and by no means destitute of a certain degree of book learning, although his reading was probably confined to old English chronicles, metrical and prose romances, and fabliaux. He also seems to have had some knowledge of the language of France. As a writer, if, as we must acknowledge,

he sometimes sinks below mediocrity, we cannot
deny that he frequently gives utterance to bursts
of genuine poetry, taking far higher flights than
his contemporaries, Richard Johnson of the
" Goulden Roses", or even Martin Parker, so
canonical in all that relates to Robin Hood.
Deloney's works exhibit the faults and excellencies
of a self-taught man, whose life, there is too great
reason to fear, was one continued struggle for
existence, and who often wrote not as fancy
willed, or the muse dictated, but because author-
ship was a worldly affair, an unpoetical matter of
pounds, shillings, and pence.   On no other
hypothesis could the author of " Fair Rosamond,"
and " The banishment of the two dukes," be the
author of " Shore's wife"; or could the author of
" The Spanish lady" (a poem which has elicited the
praises of Wordsworth) be the writer of disgusting
ballads on the executions of the poor persecuted
Catholics of his time.   Deloney was one of the
last of England's minstrel bards, and, therefore,
his publications have ever been in high esteem
amongst collectors; of several of these works, a
list is given by Mr. Collier in his preface to
Deloney's *Strange Histories* (Percy Society's
edition), but the catalogue is incomplete, and we
believe it may be extended by ascribing to Deloney
the authorship of " The Blind Beggar of Bednall
Green," and " The pleasant and sweet history of
Patient Grissel, &c.; printed by E. P. for John

Wright, dwelling in Giltspur Street, at the signe of the Bible" (see Percy Society's edition, edited by Collier); and by also ascribing to Deloney the *authorship* of the " Garland of Good-Will". The history of Patient Grissel contains a ballad extracted from the " Garland of Good-will," being the one inserted at page 82 of the present work, and of which ballad no earlier edition has been discovered. It is impossible to state when the Garland made its first appearance, but it is presumed about the year 1586: none of the original editions are known to exist, though it is not improbable that there may be such carefully concealed in the dark caverns of some of our literary Domdaniels, who, imbued with a true spirit of dog-in-the-mangerism, prevent others from tasting the food for which they themselves have no relish. The Pepysian black letter copy of the Garland is only dated 1678 (just seventy-eight years after Deloney's decease), and it is the oldest we have been enabled to consult, although we can trace two earlier editions, one of 1631, and the other of 1659. The edition of 1678 differs materially from that of 1709 (?), copies of which are neither scarce nor valuable, and are to be found in the library of the British Museum, and in the collections of Mr. James Orchard Halliwell, and others. This last-named edition, which is " printed for G. Conyers at the sign of the Golden ring in Little Britain," is in the form

of a chap-book of the commonest description, and
is printed on the coarsest paper, and with the
vilest type, and abounds in misprints, *hiati*, and
typographical blunders. The edition of 1678
bears internal evidence of being a transcript of the
original work, and it differs from Conyers' copy
in a very important particular; for while in the
latter are found several poems which are certainly
*not* by Deloney, all such interpolations are
wanting in the earlier impression. These *added*
poems are inserted in the following pages, but
the Editor has distinguished them by asterisks.
Percy, in selecting from the Garland for the
*Reliques*, has, it is clear, made use of the editions
of 1678 and 1709; for he not only gives one of
the interpolated poems from the latter, but he cor-
rects the text of the genuine ones by the readings of
the former, still further correcting that text by his
celebrated folio MS., and by conjectural emenda-
tion. (See notes to " Truth and Ignorance", and
also those to the " Spanish Lady".) In preparing
our edition of the Garland, we have printed from a
copy of Conyers' edition, lent for the purpose by
Mr. Halliwell, but the text has been collated with
the edition of 1678, and wherever any variation
has occurred, as for instance in the title-page, and
in the names of the poems, we have abided by the
readings of what we must consider as the more
authoritative copy : indeed the name of the pub-

lisher of the earlier edition is some guarantee for
its correctness; for John Wright was one of the
leading booksellers of the age, and not, as some
have erroneously asserted, a mere publisher of
ballads and penny histories, like the Marshalls
and Catnachs of the present century. The vignette
on our *old* title-page is found in both editions,
and the initial letter, at page 1, is copied from
Conyers; both of these designs have been en-
graved by George Anderson, Esq., of De Beauvoir
Town, by whom they have been presented to the
Percy Society.

The Editor intends to follow up the present
work by a republication of some of the other
Garlands mentioned, and quoted from, by Percy,
Evans, and others, *when he can discover their
whereabouts,* for he has had many an unavailing
search after them. They are *somewhere*, but
where is that somewhere? If any of those
numerous correspondents, anonymous and other-
wise, who have favoured the Editor with their
suggestions and recommendations on the subject
will be so obliging as to state how he is to reduce
them to practice, the information will be very
thankfully received. It is an easy matter to dress
your hare, but as good Mrs. Glasse says, " catch
him first".

*Tollington Villa, Hornsey,*
    *March* 1851.

THE

# GARLAND

OF

# Good-Will

## Divided into Three Parts

containing many

Pleasant SONGS and pretty POEMS,
to sundry new Notes.

With a Table to find the Names of
all the SONGS.

## Written by T. D.

## J. W.

THOV·SHALT·LABOR·TILL·THOV·RETVRNE·TO·DUST

London: Printed for J. Wright, at the sign of the
Crown, on Ludgate Hill.   1678.

# THE TABLE OF NAMES OF THE SONGS.

# TABLE OF FIRST LINES.

---

---

# GARLAND OF GOOD-WILL.

---

### THE FIRST PART.

---

### I.

### THE DEATH OF·THE FAIR LADY ROSAMOND.

To the Tune of "*Flying Fame*".

HEN as king Henry rul'd this land,
   The second of that name,
Besides the queen, he dearly lov'd
   A fair and princely dame.

Most peerless was her beauty found,
   Her favour and her face,
A sweeter creature in this world,
   Did never prince embrace.

Her crispèd locks like threads of gold
   Appear'd to each man's sight;
Her comely eyes like orient pearls,
   Did cast a heavenly light;

B

The blood within her crystal cheeks,
  Did such a colour drive,
As if the lily and the rose
  For mastership did strive.

Yea, Rosamond, fair Rosamond,
  Her name was callèd so,
To whom dame Eleanor our queen,
  Was known a mortal foe.

The king, therefore, for her defence
  Against this furious queen,
At Woodstock builded such a bower,
  The like was never seen:

Most curiously this bower was built,
  With stone and timber strong,
An hundred and fifty doors
  Did to this bower belong;

And they so cunningly contriv'd,
  With turnings round about,
That none but with a clew of thread
  Could enter in or out.

And for his love and lady's sake,
  That was so fair and bright,
The keeping of this bower he gave
  Unto a worthy knight.

But fortune that doth often frown,
   Where she before did smile,
The king's delight and lady's joy,
   Full soon she did beguile.

For why? the king's ungracious son,
   Whom he did high advance,
Against his father raisèd wars
   Within the realms of France.

And yet before our comely king,
   The English land forsook,
Of Rosamond, that lady fair,
   His last farewell he took.

O! Rosamond, the only rose
   That pleaseth best mine eye,
The fairest rose in all the world
   To feed my fantasie.

The flower of mine affected heart,
   Whose sweetness doth excel
My royal rose a thousand times,
   I bid thee now farewel.

For I must leave my famous flower,
   My sweetest Rose, a space,
And cross the seas to famous France,
   Proud rebels to abase.

But yet, my rose, be sure thou shalt
  My coming shortly see;
And in my heart, while hence I am,
  I'll bear my rose with me.


When Rosamond, that lady fair,
  Did hear the king say so,
The sorrows of her grievèd heart
  Her outward looks did show;


And from her clear and crystal eyes,
  Tears gushèd out apace,
Which, like the silver pearlèd dew,
  Ran down her comely face;


Her lips, like to the coral red,
  Did wax both wan and pale,
And for the sorrow she conceiv'd,
  Her vital spirits did fail.


And falling down all in a swound,
  Before king Henry's face,
Full oft within his princely arms
  Her body he did embrace.


And twenty times, with watry eyes,
  He kist her tender cheek,
Until he had reviv'd again
  Her senses mild and meek.

Why grieves my Rose, my sweetest Rose?
 The king did often say:
Because, quoth she, to bloody wars
 My lord must part away;

But since your grace, in foreign coasts,
 Among your foes unkind,
Must go to hazard life and limb,
 Why should I stay behind?

Nay, rather let me, like a page,
 Thy sword and target bear,
That on my breast the blow may light
 That should offend you there.

O! let me in your royal tent
 Prepare your bed at night,
And with sweet baths refresh your grace,
 At your return from fight.

So I your presence may enjoy,
 No toil I will refuse;
But wanting you my life is death,
 Which doth true love abuse.

Content thyself, my dearest love,
 Thy rest at home shall be,
In England's sweet and pleasant soil,
 For travel fits not thee.

Fair ladies brook not bloody wars,
 Sweet peace their pleasures breed;
The nourisher of heart's content,
 Which fancy first did feed.

My rose shall rest in Woodstock bower,
 With music's sweet delight;
While I among the piercing pikes
 Against my foes do fight.

My rose, in robes of pearl and gold,
 With diamonds richly dight,
Shall dance the galliard of my love,
 While I my foes do smite.

And you, Sir Thomas, whom I trust
 To be my love's defence,
Be careful of my royal rose,
 When I am parted hence.

And therewithal he fetched a sigh,
 As though his heart would break;
And Rosamond, for very grief,
 Not one plain word could speak.

And at their parting, well they might
 In heart be grievèd sore;
After that day, fair Rosamond
 The king did see no more.

And when his grace had past the seas,
  And into France had gone;
Queen Eleanor, with envious heart,
  To Woodstock came anon.

And forth she call'd this trusty knight,
  Who kept this curious bower;
Who, with this clew of twinèd thread,
  Came from this famous flower.

And when that she had wounded him,
  The queen his thread did get;
And went where lady Rosamond
  Was like an angel set.

But when the queen with steadfast eye
  Beheld her heavenly face,
She was amazèd in her mind,
  At her exceeding grace.

Cast off thy robes from thee, she said,
  That rich and costly be;
And drink thou up this deadly draught,
  Which I have brought for thee.

But presently upon her knee
  Sweet Rosamond did fall,
And pardon of the queen she crav'd
  For her offences all.

Take pity on my youthful years,
    Fair Rosamond did cry;
And let me not with poison strong
    Enforcèd be to die.

I will renounce this sinful life,
    And in a cloyster 'bide;
Or else be banish'd, if you please,
    To range the world so wide.

And for that fault which I have done,
    Though I was forc'd thereto,
Preserve my life, and punish me
    As you think good to do.

And with these words her lilly hands
    She wrung full often there;
And down along her comely face
    Proceeded many a tear.

But nothing could this furious queen
    Therewith appeasèd be;
The cup of deadly poison fill'd,
    As she sat on her knee,

She gave this comely dame to drink,
    Who took it in her hand;
And from her bended knee arose,
    And on her feet did stand;

And casting up her eyes to heaven,
　　She did for mercy call;
And drinking up the poison strong,
　　Her life she lost withal.

And when that death through every limb
　　Had done her greatest spite,
Her chiefest foes did plain confess
　　She was a glorious wight.

Her body then they did entomb,
　　When life was fled away;
At Woodstock, near to Oxford town,
　　As may be seen this day.

---

II.

## THE LAMENTATION OF SHORE'S WIFE.

To the Tune of "*The Hunt is up*".

LISTEN, fair ladies,
　　Unto my miseries,
That lived late in pomp and state most delightfully;
And now to fortune's fair dissimulation,
　　Brought in cruel and uncouth plagues most piteously.

Shore's wife I am,
　　So known by name;

And at the Flower-de-luce, in Cheapside, was my
    dwelling;
The only daughter of a wealthy merchant man,
    Against whose counsel I was evermore rebelling.

    Young was I lovèd;
    No action movèd
My heart or mind, to give or yield to their consenting,
My parent's thinking strictly for to wed me,
    Forcing me to take that which caused my repenting.

    Then being wedded,
    I was quickly tempted;
My beauty causèd many gallants to salute me.
The king commanded, and I straight obeyèd;
    For his chiefest jewel then he did repute me.

    Bravely was I trainèd,
    Like a queen I reignèd,
And poor men's suits by me were obtainèd.
In all the court, to none was such great resort,
    As unto me, though now in scorn I be disdainèd.

    When the king dièd,
    My grief was trièd;
From the court I was expellèd with despight.
The duke of Gloucester, being lord protector,
    Took away my goods against all law and right.

    And a procession,
    For my transgression,

Bare-footed he made me go for to shame me ;
A cross before me there was carried plainly,
  As a penance to my former life for to tame me.


  Then through London,
    Being thus undone,
The lord protector published a proclamation,
On pain of death I should not be harbour'd ;
  Which furthermore encreas'd my sorrow and vexation.


  I that had plenty,
    And dishes dainty,
Most sumptuously brought to my board at my pleasure ;
Being full poor, from door to door
  I beg my bread with clack and dish at my leisure.


  My rich attire,
    By fortune's ire,
To rotten rags and nakedness they are beaten.
My body soft, which the king embracèd oft,
  With vermin vile annoy'd and eat on.


  On stalls and stones,
    Did lie my bones,
That wonted was in bed of down to be placèd :
And you see my finest pillows be
  Of stinking straw, with dirt and dung thus disgracèd.


  Wherefore, fair ladies,
    With your sweet babies,

My grievous fall bear in your mind, and behold me :
How strange a thing, that the love of a king
  Should come to die under a stall, as I told ye.

---

### III.

### A SONG OF KING EDGAR, SHEWING HOW HE WAS DECEIVED OF HIS LOVE, &c.

To the Tune of " *Labandulishot*".

WHEN as king Edgar did govern this land,
    Adown, adown, down, down, down,
And in the strength of his years he did stand,
    Call him down-a ;
Such praise was spread of a gallant dame,
Which did through England carry great fame ;
And she a lady of high degree,
The earl of Devonshire's daughter was she.
The king, which lately had bury'd the queen,
And not long time a widower been,
Hearing this praise of a gallant maid,
Upon her beauty his love he laid ;
And in his mind he would often say,
I will send for that lady gay ;
Yea, I will send for this lady bright,
Which is my treasure and delight ;
Whose beauty, like to Phœbus' beams,

Doth glitter through all christian realms.
Then to himself he would reply;
Saying, how fond a prince am I,
To cast my love so base and low,
Upon a girl I do not know!
King Edgar will his fancy frame
To love some peerless princely dame,
The daughter of a royal king,
That may a dainty dowry bring:
Whose matchless beauty, brought in place,
May Estrild's colour clean disgrace.
But, senseless man, what do I mean,
Upon a broken reed to lean?
Or what fond fury did me move,
Thus to abuse my dearest love?
Whose visage, grac'd with heavenly hue,
Doth Ellen's honour quite subdue.
The glory of her beauteous pride,
Sweet Estrild's father doth deride.
Then pardon my unseemly speech,
Dear love and lady, I beseech,
For I my thoughts will henceforth frame,
To spread the honour of thy name.
Then unto him he call'd a knight,
Which was most trusty in his sight,
And unto him thus did he say,
To earl Orgator, Go thy way,
Where ask for Estrild, comely dame,
Whose beauty went so far by fame;
And if you find her comely grace,

As fame did spread in every place;
Then tell her father she shall be
My crownèd queen, if she agree.
The knight in message did proceed,
And into Devonshire went with speed;
But when he saw the lady bright,
He was so ravisht at her sight,
That nothing could his passion move,
Except he might obtain her love.
For day and night while there he staid,
He courted still this peerless maid;
And in his suit he shew'd such skill,
That at the length he gain'd her good-will;
Forgetting quite the duty tho'
Which he unto the king did owe.
Then coming home unto his grace,
He told him with dissembling face,
That those reporters were to blame,
That so advanc'd the maiden's name:
For I assure your grace, said he,
She is as other women be;
Her beauty, of such great report,
No better than the common sort;
And far unmeet in every thing,
To match with such a noble king.
But though her face be nothing fair,
Yet sith she is her father's heir,
Perhaps some lord of high degree
Would very fain her husband be.
Then if your grace would give consent,

I would myself be well content
The damsel for my wife to take,
For her great lands' and livings' sake.
The king, whom thus he did deceive,
Incontinent did give him leave;
For on this point he did not stand;
For why? he had not need of land.
Then being glad he went away,
And wedded straight this lady gay.
The fairest creature bearing life,
Had this false knight unto his wife;
And by that match of high degree,
An earl soon after that was he.
Ere he long time had married been,
That many had her beauty seen,
Her praise was spread both far and near;
The king again thereof did hear;
Who then in heart did plainly prove
He was betrayèd of his love:
Though, therefore, he was vexèd sore,
Yet seem'd he not to grieve therefore;
But kept his count'nance good and kind,
As though he bore no grudge in mind.
But on a day it came to pass,
When as the king full merry was,
To Ethelwold in sport, he said,
I muse what chear there should be made,
If to thy house I should resort
A night or two for princely sport?
Hereat the earl shew'd count'nance glad,

Though in his heart he was full sad;
Saying, your grace shall welcome be,
If so your grace will honour me.
Then as the day appointed was,
Before the king did thither pass,
The earl before hand did prepare
The king his coming to declare.
And with a count'nance passing grim,
He call'd his lady unto him;
Saying, with sad and heavy cheer,
I pray you, when the king comes here,
Sweet lady, as you tender me,
Let your attire but homely be;
Nor wash not thou thy angel's face,
But so thy beauty clean disgrace;
Thereto thy gesture so apply,
It may seem loathsome to the eye,
For if the king should there behold
Thy glorious beauty so extoll'd,
Then shall my life soon shorten'd be,
For my deserts and treachery.
When to thy father first I came,
Though I did not declare the same,
Yet was I put in trust to bring
The joyful tidings to the king;
Who, for thy glorious beauty seen,
Did think of thee to make his queen.
But when I had thy person found,
Thy beauty gave me such a wound,
No rest nor comfort could I take.

Till you, sweet love, my grief did slake;
And tho' that duty chargèd me,
Most faithful to my lord to be,
Yet love, upon the other side,
Bid for my self I should provide.
Then for my suit and service shown,
At length I won you for my own:
And for my love in wedlock spent,
Your choice you need no whit repent:
Then since my grief I have expresst,
Sweet lady, grant me my request.
Good words she gave with smiling chear,
Musing of that which she did hear;
And casting many things in mind,
Great fault therewith she seem'd to find;
But in her self she thought it shame,
To make that foul which God did frame.
Most costly robes full rich therefore,
In bravest sort that day she wore;
Doing all that e'er she might,
To set her beauty forth to sight:
And her best skill in every thing
She shew'd to entertain the king.
Wherefore the king so 'snarèd was,
That reason quite from him did pass:
His heart by her was set on fire,
He had to her a great desire;
And for the looks he gave her then,
For every look she shew'd him ten.
Wherefore the king perceivèd plain,

His love and looks were not in vain.
Upon a time it chancèd so,
The king he would a hunting go;
And as they through a wood did ride,
The earl on horse-back by his side,
For so the story telleth plain,
That with a shaft the earl was slain.
So that when he had lost his life,
He took the lady unto wife;
Who married her, all harm to shun,
By whom he did beget a son.
Thus he that did the king deceive,
Did by desert his death receive:
Then to conclude and make an end,
Be true and faithful to thy friend.

---

### IV.

#### HOW COVENTRY WAS MADE FREE BY GODINA, COUNTESS OF CHESTER.

To the Tune of " *Prince Arthur died at Ludlow*", &c.

LEOFRICUS, that noble earl
  Of Chester, as I read,
Did for the city of Coventry
  Many a noble deed.

Great privileges for the town
  This noble man did get;
And of all things did make it so,
  That they toll-free did sit.

Save only that for horses still
   They did some custom pay,
Which was great charges to the town,
   Full long and many a day.

Wherefore his wife Godina fair,
   Did of the earl request,
That therefore he would make it free,
   As well as all the rest.

So when that she long time had sued,
   Her purpose to obtain,
Her noble lord at length she took
   Within a pleasant vein :

And unto him with smiling chear,
   She did forthwith proceed,
Entreating greatly that he would
   Perform that goodly deed.

You move me much, my fair, quoth he,
   Your suit I fain would shun ;
But what will you perform and do,
   To have this matter done ?

Why any thing, my lord (quoth she),
   You will with reason crave ;
I will perform it with good will,
   If I my wish might have.

If thou wilt grant the thing, he said,
  What I shall now require,
As soon as it is finishèd,
  Thou shalt have thy desire.

Command what you think good, my lord,
  I will thereto agree,
On this condition : that the town
  For ever may be free.

If thou wilt thy cloaths strip off,
  And hereby lay them down,
And at noon-day on horse-back ride
  Stark naked through the town,

They shall be free for evermore :
  If thou wilt not do so,
More liberty than now they have
  I never will bestow.

The lady at this strange demand,
  Was much abasht in mind ;
And yet for to fulfil this thing,
  She never a whit repin'd.

Wherefore unto all officers
  Of the town she sent,
That they perceiving her good will,
  Which for the weal was bent ;

That on the day that she should ride,
  All persons through the town,
Should keep their houses, shut their doors,
  And clap their windows down;

So that no creature, young or old,
  Should in the streets be seen,
Till she had ridden all about,
  Throughout the city clean.

And when the day of riding came,
  No person did her see,
Saving her lord; after which time,
  The town was ever free.

---

v.

## OF THE DUKE OF CORNWAL'S DAUGHTER.

To the Tune of "*In Greece*".

WHEN Humber, in his wrathful rage,
  King Albanack in field had slain;
Whose bloody broils for to asswage,
  King Locrin then apply'd his pain;
And with a host of Britons stout,
At length he found king Humber out.

At vantage great he met him then,
  And with his host beset him so,
That he destroy'd his warlike men,
  And Humber's power did overthrow;

And Humber, which for fear did fly,
Leapt into a river desp'rately:

And being drownèd in the deep,
   He left a lady there alive,
Which sadly did lament and weep,
   For fear they should her life deprive.
But by her face, that was so fair,
The king was caught in Cupid's snare.

He took this lady to his love,
   Who secretly did keep it still,
So that the queen did quickly prove
   The king did bear her much good-will.
Which though by wedlock late begun,
He had by her a gallant son.

Queen Guendoline was griev'd in mind
   To see the king was alter'd so;
At length the cause she chanc'd to find,
   Which brought her to most bitter woe.
For Estrild was his joy (God wot),
By whom a daughter he begot.

The duke of Cornwal being dead,
   The father of that gallant queen,
The king with lust being overlaid,
   His lawful wife he cast off clean:
Who, with her dear and tender son,
For succour did in Cornwal run.

Then Locrin crownèd Estrild bright,
  And made of her his lawful wife ;
With her, which was his heart's delight,
  He sweetly thought to lead his life.
Thus Guendoline, as one forlorn,
Did hold her wretched life in scorn.

But when the Cornish men did know
  The great abuse she did endure,
With her a number great did go,
  Which she by prayer did procure.
In battel then they marcht along,
For to redress this grievous wrong ;

And near a river callèd Store,
  The king with all his host she met ;
Where both the armies fought full sore,
  But yet the queen the field did get.
Yet ere they did the conquest gain,
The king was with an arrow slain.

Then Guendoline did take in hand,
  Until her son was come to age,
The government of all the land.
  But first her fury to asswage,
She did command her soldiers wild,
To drown both Estrild and her child.

Incontinent then did they bring
  Fair Estrild to the river side,

And Sabrine, daughter to a king,
   Whom Guendoline could not abide :
Who, being bound together fast,
Into the river there were cast :

And ever since, that running stream,
   Wherein the ladies drownèd were,
Is callèd Savern through the realm,
   Because that Sabrine dièd there.
Thus those that did to lewdness bend,
Were brought unto a woful end.

-------

### VI.

## A SONG OF QUEEN ISABEL, WIFE TO KING EDWARD THE SECOND, WITH THE DOWN-FALL OF THE SPENCERS.

PROUD were the Spencers, and of condition ill,
All England, and the king likewise, they rulèd at their
    will :
And many lords and nobles of the land,
Through their occasions lost their lives, and none did
    them withstand.

And at the last they did encrease much grief,
Between the king and Isabel, his queen and faithful
    wife ;
So that her life she dreaded wondrous sore,
And cast within her secret thoughts some present help
    therefore.

Then she requests, with count'nance grave and sage,
That she to Thomas Becket's tomb might go on
    pilgrimage;
Then being joyful to have that happy chance,
Her son and she took ships with speed, and sailèd into
    France.

And royally she was receivèd then
By the king and all the rest of peers and noblemen;
And unto him at last she did express
The cause of her arrival there, her cause and heaviness.

When as her brother her grief did understand,
He gave her leave to gather men throughout this
    famous land;
And made a promise to aid her evermore,
As often as she should stand in need of gold and silver
    store.

But when indeed she did require the same,
He was as far from doing it as when she thither came;
And did proclaim, whilst matters were so seen,
That none, on pain of death, should go to aid the
    English queen.

This alteration did greatly grieve the queen,
That down along her comely face the bitter tears were
    seen.
When she perceiv'd her friends forsook her so,
She knew not for her safety which way to turn or go.

But through good hap, at last she then decreed
To seek in fruitful Germany some succour to this need :
And to Sir John Hainault then went she,
Who entertain'd this woeful queen with great solemnity.

And with great sorrow to him she then complain'd,
Of all her griefs and injuries which she of late sustain'd.
So that with weeping she dimm'd her princely sight,
The cause whereof did greatly grieve that noble
    courteous knight;

Who made an oath he would her champion be,
And in her quarrel spend his blood, from wrong to set
    her free;
And all my friends, with whom I may prevail,
Shall help for to advance your state, whose truth no
    time shall fail.

And in his promise most faithful he was found,
And many lords of great account were in his voyage
    bound.
So setting forward with a goodly train,
At length, through God's especial grace, into England
    they came.

At Harwich then, when they were ashore,
Of English lords and barons bold there came to her
    great store;
Which did rejoice the queen's afflicted heart,
That English lords in such sort came for to take her
    part.

When as king Edward thereof did understand,
How that the queen with such a power was enter'd on
    his land;
And how his nobles were gone to take her part,
He fled from London presently, even with a heavy
    heart.

And with the Spencers unto Bristol did go,
To fortifie that gallant town great cost he did bestow;
Leaving behind, to govern London town,
The stout bishop of Exeter, whose pride was soon
    pull'd down.

The Mayor of London, with citizens great store,
The bishop, and the Spencers both, in heart they did
    abhor;
Therefore they took him without fear or dread,
And at the Standard, in Cheapside, they smote off his
    head.

Unto the queen this message then they sent,
The city of London was at her commandement.
Wherefore the queen, with all her company,
Did strait to Bristol march amain, whereat the king did
    lie.

Then she besiegèd the city round about,
Threatning sharp and cruel death to those that were so
    stout;
Wherefore the townsmen, their children, and their
    wives,

Did yield the city to the queen, for safeguard of their
    lives.

Where was took, the story plain doth tell,
Sir Hugh Spencer, and with him the Earl of Arundel.
This judgment just, the nobles did set down;
They should be drawn and hangèd, both, in sight of
    Bristol town.

Then was king Edward in the castle there,
And Hugh Spencer still with him, in dread and deadly
    fear;
And being prepar'd from thence to sail away,
The winds were found contrary, they were enforc'd to
    stay.

But at last Sir John Beaumont, knight,
Did bring his sailing ship to shore, and so did stay
    their flight.
And so these men were taken speedily
And brought as prisoners to the queen who did in Bristol
    lie.

The queen, by counsel of the lords and barons bold,
To Barkley sent the king, there to be kept in hold:
And young Hugh Spencer, that did much ill procure,
Was to the marshal of the host sent unto keeping sure.

And then the queen to Hereford took her way,
With all her warlike company, which late in Bristol lay:

And here behold how Spencer was,
From town to town, even as the queen to Hereford did
    pass :

Upon a jade, which they by chance had found,
Young Spencer mounted was, with legs and hands fast
    bound :
A writing paper along as he did go,
Upon his head he had to wear, which did his treason
    show ;

And to deride this traytor lewd and ill,
Certain men with reeden pipes, did blow before him still ;
Thus was he led along in every place,
While many people did rejoyce, to see his strange
    disgrace.

When unto Hereford our noble queen was come,
She did assemble all the lords and knights, both all
    and some ;
And in their presence young Spencer judgment had,
To be both hang'd and quarterèd, his treasons were so
    bad ;

Then was the king deposèd of his crown,
From rule, and princely dignity, the lords did cast him
    down :
And in his life, his son both wise and sage,
Was crown'd king of fair England, at fifteen years of
    age.

## VII

## A SONG OF THE BANISHMENT OF THE TWO DUKES OF HEREFORD AND NORFOLK.

Two noble dukes of great renown,
 That long had liv'd in fame,
Through hateful envy were cast down,
 And brought to sudden shame.

The duke of Hereford was the one,
 A prudent prince and wise,
'Gainst whom such malice there was shown,
 Which soon in fight did rise.

The duke of Norfolk, most untrue,
 Declar'd unto the king,
The duke of Hereford greatly grew
 In hatred of each thing,

Which by his grace was acted still,
 Against both high and low;
How he had a trait'rous will
 His state to overthrow.

The duke of Hereford, then in haste,
 Was sent for to the king;
And by the lords in order plac'd,
 Examin'd of each thing.

Who being guiltless of this crime,
   Which was against him laid,
The duke of Norfolk at that time,
   These words unto him said:

How canst thou, with a shameless face,
   Deny a truth so stout;
And here before his royal grace,
   So falsly face it out?

Did not these wicked treasons pass,
   When we together were,
How that the king unworthy was,
   The royal crown to bear?

Wherefore, my gracious lord, quoth he,
   And you his noble peers,
To whom I wish long life to be,
   With many happy years;

I do pronounce before you all,
   This treacherous lord that's here;
A traytor to our noble king,
   As time shall shew it clear.

The duke of Hereford hearing that,
   In mind was grievèd much,
And did return this answer flat,
   Which did duke Norfolk touch.

The term of traytor, truthless duke,
  In scorn and great disdain,
With flat defiance to thy face
  I do return again.

And therefore, if it please your grace
  To grant me leave, quoth he,
To combate with my unknown foe
  That here accuseth me;

. I do not doubt, but plainly prove,
  That like a perjured knight,
He hath most falsly sought my shame,
  Against all truth and right.

The king did grant this just request,
  And did therewith agree,
At Coventry, in August next,
  This combate fought should be.

The dukes on sturdy steeds full stout,
  In coats of steel most bright,
With spears in rests, did enter lists,
  This combate fierce to fight.

The king then cast his warder down,
  Commanding them to stay;
And with his lords he counsel took,
  To stint that mortal fray.

At length unto these noble dukes
   The king of heraulds came,
And unto them with lofty speech
   This sentence did proclaim:

Sir Henry Bullenbrook, this day,
   The duke of Hereford here,
And Thomas Mauberry, Norfolk duke,
   So valiantly did appear;

And having, in honourable sort,
   Repairèd to this place,
Our noble king, for special cause,
   Had alter'd thus the case.

First, Henry, duke of Hereford,
   Ere fifteen days be past,
Shall part the realm on pain of death,
   While ten years' space doth last.

And Thomas, duke of Norfolk now,
   That hath begun this strife,
And thereof no good proof can bring,
   I say for term of life;

By judgment of our soveraign lord,
   Which now in place doth stand,
For evermore I banish thee
   Out of thy native land.

D

Charging thee, on pain of death,
   When fifteen days are past,
Thou never tread on English ground
   So long as life doth last.

Thus they were sworn before the king,
   Ere they did further pass,
The one should never come in place,
   Where as the other was.

Then both the dukes, with heavy hearts,
   Were parted presently,
The uncouth streams of froward chance,
   Of foreign lands to try.

The duke of Norfolk coming then,
   Where he would shipping take,
The bitter tears ran down his cheeks,
   And thus his moan did make:

Now let me sigh and sob my fill,
   Ere I from hence depart,
That inward pangs with speed may burst
   My sore afflicted heart.

Oh cursed man! whose loathèd life
   Is held so much in scorn,
Whose company is clean despis'd,
   And left as one forlorn,

Now take thy leave and last adieu
  Of this thy country dear,
Which never more thou must behold,
  Nor yet approach it near.

Happy should I account my self,
  If death my heart had torn;
That I might have my bones entomb'd
  Where I was bred and born.

Or that by Neptune's wrathful rage,
  I might be prest to die,
Whilst that sweet England's pleasant banks
  Did stand before mine eye.

How sweet a scent hath English ground
  Within my senses now!
How fair unto my outward sight
  Seem every branch and bough!

The fields and flowers, the streets and stones,
  Seem such unto my mind,
That in all other countries sure
  The like I ne'er shall find.

O! that the sun, with shining face,
  Would stay his steed by strength,
That this same day might stretchèd be
  To twenty years in length;

And that the true-performing tyde
  Her hasty course would stay;
That Eolus would never yield
  To bear me hence away.

That by the fountain of my eyes
  The fields might water'd be;
That I might grave my grievous plaint
  Upon each springing tree.

But time, I see, with eagle's wings,
  So swift doth fly away,
And dusky clouds begin to dim
  The brightness of the day.

The fatal hour draweth on,
  The winds and tydes agree;
And now, sweet England, oversoon,
  I must depart from thee.

The mariners have hoised sail,
  And call to catch me in;
And now in woeful heart I feel
  My torments to begin.

Wherefore, farewel for evermore,
  Sweet England, unto thee;
But farewel, all my friends, which I
  Again shall never see.

And, England, here I kiss thy ground,
　Upon my bended knee,
Whereby to shew to all the world
　How dearly I love thee.

This being said, away he went,
　As fortune did him guide:
And at the length with grief of heart
　In Venice there he dy'd.

The noble duke in doleful sort
　Did lead his life in France;
And at the last the mighty lord
　Did him full high advance.

The lords of England afterwards
　Did send for him again;
While that king Richard at the wars
　In Ireland did remain.

Who, by the vile and great abuse,
　Which through his deeds did spring,
Deposèd was; and then the duke
　Was truly crownèd king.

## VIII

# THE NOBLE ACTS OF ARTHUR, OF THE ROUND TABLE, AND OF LANCELOT DU LAKE.

To the Tune of "*Flying Fame*".

WHEN Arthur first in court began,
  And was approvèd king,
By force of arms great victories won,
  And conquests home did bring;

Then into Britain straight he came,
  Where fifty good and able
Knights then repairèd unto him,
  Which were of the Round Table;

And many justs and tournaments
  Before them there were drest,
Where valiant knights did then excel,
  And far surmount the rest.

But one Sir Lancelot du Lake,
  Who was approvèd well,
He in his fights and deeds of arms,
  All others did excel.

When he had rested him a while,
  To play, to game, and sport,
He thought he would go try himself,
  In some adven'trous sort.

He armèd rode in forest wide,
  And met a damsel fair,
Who told him of adventures great,
  Whereto he gave good ear.

Why should I not? quoth Lancelot, tho'
  For that cause I came hither.
Thou seem'st, quoth she, a goodly knight,
  And I will bring thee thither,

Whereas the mighty knight doth dwell,
  That now is of great fame;
Therefore tell me what knight thou art,
  And then what is your name?

My name is Lancelot du Lake.
  Quoth she, it likes me than;
Here dwells a knight that never was
  E'er match'd with any man;

Who has in prison threescore knights,
  And four that he has bound;
Knights of king Arthur's court they be,
  And of his Table Round.

She brought him to a river side,
  And also to a tree,
Whereon a copper bason hung,
  His fellow shields to see.

He struck so hard, the bason broke :
   When Tarquin heard the sound,
He drove a horse before him straight,
   Whereon a knight lay bound.

Sir knight, then said Sir Lancelot,
   Bring me that horse-load hither,
And lay him down, and let him rest ;
   We'll try our force together.

And as I understand thou hast,
   So far as thou art able,
Done great despite and shame unto
   The knights of the Round Table.

If thou be of the Table Round,
   (Quoth Tarquin, speedilye),
Both thee and all thy fellowship
   I utterly defie.

That's overmuch, quoth Lancelot though ;
   Defend thee by and by.
They put their spurs unto their steeds,
   And each at other fly.

They coucht their spears, and horses ran,
   As though there had been thunder :
And each struck them amidst the shield,
   Wherewith they broke in sunder.

Their horses' backs brake under them,
　　The knights were both astound;
To 'void their horses, they made great haste
　　To light upon the ground.

They took them to their shields full fast,
　　Their swords they drew out than;
With mighty strokes most eagerly
　　Each one at other ran.

They wounded were, and bled full sore,
　　For breath they both did stand,
And leaning on their swords awhile,
　　Quoth Tarquin, Hold thy hand!

And tell to me what I shall ask:
　　Say on, quoth Lancelot though;
Thou art, quoth Tarquin, the best knight
　　That ever I did know,

And like a knight that I did hate;
　　So that thou be not he,
I will deliver all the rest,
　　And eke accord with thee.

That is well said, quoth Lancelot, then,
　　But sith it must be so,
What is the knight thou hatest so,
　　I pray thee to me show?

His name is Lancelot du Lake,
  He slew my brother dear;
Him I suspect of all the rest;
  I would I had him here.


Thy wish thou hast, but yet unknown;
  I am Lancelot du Lake!
Now knight of Arthur's Table Round,
  Kind Haud's son of Seuwake;


And I desire thee do thy worst:
  Ho! ho! quoth Tarquin though,
One of us two shall end our lives
  Before that we do go.


If thou be Lancelot du Lake,
  Then welcome shalt thou be;
Wherefore see thou thyself defend,
  For now defie I thee.


They buckled then together so,
  Like two wild boars rashing,
And with their swords and shields they ran
  At one another flashing.


The ground besprinkled was with blood,
  Tarquin began to faint;
For he gave back, and bore his shield,
  So low, he did repent.

This soon 'spied Sir Lancelot though,
  He leapt upon him then,
He pull'd him down upon his knee,
  And, rushing off his helm,

And then he struck his neck in two;
  And when he had done so,
From prison, threescore knights and four
  Lancelot deliverèd though.

———

IX.

A SONG IN PRAISE OF WOMEN.

To a pleasant new Tune, called, " *My Valentine*".

AMONG all other things
That God hath made beneath the sky,
Most glorious to satisfie the curious eye
  Of mortal men withal,
  The sight of Eve,
  Did soonest fit his fancy;
Whose courtesie and amity most speedily
  Had caught his heart in thrall;
  Whom he did love so dear,
  As plainly doth appear,
He made her queen of all the world, and mistress of
    his heart;
Tho' afterwards she wrought his woe, his death
    and deadly smart.

What need I speak
Of matters passèd long ago ?
Which all men know I need not show, to high or low,
 The case it is so plain :
 Altho' that Eve
 Committed then so great offence,
Ere she went hence, a recompence, in defence,
 She made mankind again :
 For by her blessed seed,
 We are redeem'd indeed.
Why should not then all mortal men esteem of
 women well ?
And love their wives, even as their lives, as nature
 doth compel ?


 A virtuous wife
 The scripture doth commend ; and say,
That night and day, she is a stay from all decay,
 To keep her husband still ;
 She useth not
 To give herself a wandring,
Or flattering, or prattling, or any thing
 To do her neighbour ill ;
 But all her mind is bent,
 His pleasure to content ;
Her faithful love doth not remove for any storm or
 grief ;
Then is he not well blest, think ye, that meets with
 such a wife ?

But now methinks
I hear some men do say to me,
Few such there be, in each degree and quality
At this day to be found;
And now-a-days
Some men do set their whole delight,
Both day and night, with all despite, to brawl and
fight,
Their rage doth so abound:
But sure I think and say,
Here comes no such to day;
Nor do I know of any she, that is within this place,
And yet for fear, I dare not swear, it is so hard a
case.

But to conclude;
For maids, and wives, and virgins all,
Both great or small, in bower or hall, to pray I shall,
So long as life doth last,
That they may live,
With heart's content, and perfect peace,
That joy's increase may never cease, till death
release
The care that crept so fast:
For beauty doth me bind,
To have them all in mind;
Even for her sake, that doth us make so merry to be
seen,
The glory of the female kind, I mean our noble
queen.

x.

## A SONG IN PRAISE OF A SINGLE LIFE.

To the Tune of " *The Ghost's Hearse* ".

SOME do write of bloody wars,
　　Some do shew the several jars
'Twixt men, through envy raisèd ;
　　Some in praise of princes write,
　　Some set their whole delight
To hear fair beauty blazèd :
　　Some other persons are movèd
　　For to praise where they are lovèd :
　　And let lovers praise beauty as they will,
Otherways I am intended :
　　True love is little regarded,
　　And often goes unrewarded :
　　Then to avoid all strife,
　　I'll resolve to lead a single life,
Whereby the heart is not offended.


　　O what a suit and service too
　　Is used by them that woo !
　　O what grief in heart and mind,
　　What sorrow we do find,
Through woman's fond behaviour !
　　Subject to suffer each hour,
　　And speeches sharp and sour,
　　And labour, love, and cost,
　　Perchance 'tis but all lost,

And no way to be amended ;
    And so purchase pleasure,
    And after repent at leisure.
      Then to avoid all strife, &c.

    To man in wedded state,
    Doth happen much debate,
Except by God's special favour ;
    If his wife be proudly bent,
    Or secretly consent
To any lewd behaviour :
    If she be slothful or idle,
    Or such as her tongue cannot bridle,
    Oh ! then well were he,
    If death his bane would be ;
No sorrow else can be amended ;
    For look how long he were living,
    Evermore he would be grieving.
      Then to avoid all strife, &c.

    Married folks we often hear,
    Even through their children dear,
Have many causes of sorrows,
    If disobedient they be found,
    Or false in any ground,
By their unlawful forays ;
    To see such wicked fellows,
    Shamefully come unto the gallows,
    Whom parents with great care,
    Nourishèd with dainty fare,

From their birth truly tended;
    When as their mothers before them,
    Do curse the day that e'er they bore them.
      Then to avoid all strife, &c.


    Do we then behold and see,
    When men and wives agree,
And live together,
    Where the Lord hath sent them eke
    Fair children mild and meek,
Like flowers in summer weather;
    How greatly are they grievèd,
    And will not by joy be relievèd;
    If that death doth call,
    Either wife or children small,
Whom their virtues do commend;
    Their losses whom they thus lovèd,
    From their hearts cannot be movèd.
      Then to avoid all strife, &c.


    Who being in that happy state,
    Would work himself such hate,
His fancy for to follow?
    Or, living here devoid of strife,
    Would take to him a wife,
For to procure his sorrow?
    With carping and with caring,
    Evermore must be sparing;
    Were he not worse than mad,
    Being merry, would be sad?

Were he to be commended,
    That e'er would seek much pleasure,
    Where grief is all his treasure?
    Then to avoid all strife, &c.

---

### XI.

### THE WIDDOW'S SOLACE.

To the Tune of "*Robinson Almain.*"

MOURN no more, fair widdow,
    Thy tears are all in vain;
'Tis neither grief nor sorrow,
    Can call the dead again:
Man's well enough compared
    Unto the summer's flower,
Which now is fair and pleasant,
    Yet withereth in an hour:
And mourn no more in vain,
    As one whose faith is small;
Be patient in affliction,
    And give God thanks for all.

All men are born to die,
    The scripture telleth plain:
Of earth we were created,
    To earth we must again;
'Twas not Crœsus' treasure,
    Nor Alexander's fame,

Nor Solomon by wisdom,
    That could death's fury tame;
No physick might preserve them,
    When nature did decay;
What man can hold for ever,
    The thing that will away?
        Then mourn no more, &c.


Though you have lost your husband,
    Your comfort in distress;
Consider God regardeth
    The widdow's heaviness:
And hath strictly chargèd,
    Such as his children be,
The fatherless and widdow
    To shield from injury.
        Then mourn no more, &c.


If he were true and faithful,
    And loving unto thee,
Doubt not but there's in England,
    Enough as good as he;
But if that such affection,
    Within his heart was none,
Then give God praise and glory,
    That he is dead and gone.
        And mourn no more, &c.


Receive such suitors friendly,
    As do resort to thee;

Respect not the outward person,
　But the inward gravity :
And with advisèd judgment,
　Chuse him above the rest,
Whom thou by proof hast tried,
　And found to be the best.
　　Then mourn no more, &c.


Then shalt thou live a life
　Exempt from all annoy ;
And whensoever it chanceth,
　I pray God give thee joy.
And thus I make an end,
　With true humility ;
In hope my simple solace
　May well accepted be.
　　Then mourn no more, &c.

---

### XII.

### A GENTLEWOMAN'S COMPLAINT AGAINST HER
### FAITHLESS FRIEND, &c.

FAITH is a figure standing now for nought ;
Faith is a fancy we ought to cast in thought ;
Faith now-a-days, as all the world may see,
Resteth in few, and faith is fled from thee.

Is there any faith in strangers to be found ?
Is there any faith lies hidden in the ground ?

E 2

Is there any faith in men that buried be?
No, there is none; and faith is fled from thee.

Fled is the faith that might remain in any;
Fled is the faith that should remain in many;
Fled is the faith that should in any be;
Then farewel hope, for faith is fled from thee.

From faith I see that all things are a dying;
From faith I see that every one is flying;
They from faith, that most in faith should be,
And faithless thou, that brake thy faith to me.

Thee have I sought, but thee I could not find;
Thou of all others most within my mind;
Thee have I left, and I alone will be,
Because I find that faith is fled from thee.

---

### XIII.

### HOW A PRINCE OF ENGLAND WOOED THE KING'S DAUGHTER OF FRANCE, AND HOW SHE WAS MARRIED TO A FORRESTER.

To the Tune of " *Crimson Velvet*".

IN the days of old,
    When fair France did flourish,
Stories plainly told,
    Lovers felt annoy;
The king a daughter had,
    Beauteous, fair, and lovely,

Which made her father glad,
  She was his only joy.
A prince of England came,
Whose deeds did merit fame,
  He woo'd her long, and lo! at last,
Took what he did require;
She granted his desire,
  Their hearts in one were linkèd fast.
Which when her father provèd,
Lord! how he was movèd
  And tormented in his mind:
He sought for to prevent them,
And to discontent them;
  Fortune crosses lovers kind.
When as these princely twain
  Were thus debarr'd of pleasure,
Through the king's disdain,
  Which their joys withstood,
The lady lockt up close
  Her jewels and her treasure,
Having no remorse
  Of state or royal blood.
In homely poor array,
She went to court away,
  To meet her love and heart's delight;
Who in a forest great,
Had taken up his seat
  To wait her coming in the night.
But lo! what sudden danger,
To this princely stranger,

Chancèd as he sat alone;
By outlaws he was robbèd,
And with poinard stabbèd,
   Uttering many a dying groan ;
The princess armèd by him,
   And by true desire,
Wandering all that night,
   Without dread at all :
Still unknown, she past
   In her strange attire,
Coming at the last
   Within echo's call.
You, fair woods, quoth she,
Honourèd may you be,
   Harbouring my heart's delight ;
Which doth encompass here,
My joy and only dear,
   My trusty friend, and comely knight ?
Sweet ! I come unto thee,
Sweet ! I come to wooe thee,
   That thou may'st not angry be ;
For my long delaying,
And thy courteous staying,
   Amends for all I make to thee.
Passing thus alone,
   Through the silent forest
Many a grievous groan
   Sounded in her ear ;
Where she heard a man
   To lament the sorest

Chance that ever came,
  Forc'd by deadly fear;
Farewel! my dear, quoth he,
Whom I shall never see;
  For why? my life is at an end;
For thy sweet sake I die,
Through villain's cruelty,
  To shew I am a faithful friend;
Here lie I a-bleeding,
While my thoughts are feeding
  On the rarest beauty found;
O! hard hap that may be,
Little knows my lady
  My heart-blood lies on the ground.
With that he gave a groan,
  That did break asunder
All the tender strings
  Of his gentle heart;
She who knew his voice,
  At his tale did wonder;
All her former joys
  Did to grief convert;
Straight she ran to see,
Who this man should be,
  That so like her love did speak;
And found when as she came,
Her lovely lord lay slain,
  Smeer'd in blood, which life did break:
Which when that she espied,
Lord! how sore she cried,

Her sorrows could not counted be;
Her eyes like fountains running,
While she cryed out, My darling,
Would God that I had dy'd for thee!
His pale lips, alas!
Twenty times she kissèd,
And his face did wash
With her brinish tears;
Every bleeding wound,
Her fair face bedewèd;
Wiping off the blood
With her golden hairs.
Speak, fair prince, to me;
One sweet word of comfort give;
Lift up thy fair eyes,
Listen to my cries;
Think in what great grief I live.
All in vain she suèd;
All in vain she wooed;
The prince's life was fled and gone:
There stood she still mourning,
Till the sun's returning,
And bright day was coming on.
In this great distress,
Quoth this royal lady,
Who can now express
What will become of me?
To my father's court
Never will I wander,
But some service seek,

Where I may placèd be.
Whilst she thus made her moan,
Weeping all alone,
  In this deep and deadly fear,
A forester, all in green,
Most comely to be seen,
  Ranging the wood did find her there,
Round beset with sorrow;
Maid! quoth he, good morrow;
  What hard hap hath brought you here?
Harder hap did never
Chance to a maiden ever;
  Here lies slain my brother dear:
Where might I be plac'd,
  Gentle forester, tell me?
Where might I procure
  A service in my need?
Pains I will not spare,
  But will do my duty;
Ease me of my care,
  Help my extream need.
The forester all amazèd,
On her beauty gazèd,
  'Till his heart was set on fire:
If, fair maid, quoth he,
You will go with me,
  You shall have your heart's desire.
He brought her to his mother,
And above all other,
  He set forth this maiden's praise:

Long was his heart inflamèd,
At length her love he gainèd,
   So fortune did his glory raise.
Thus unknown, he matcht
   With the king's fair daughter;
Children seven he had,
   Ere she to him was known;
But when he understood
   She was a royal princess,
By this means, at last,
   He shewèd forth her fame.
He cloath'd his children then,
Not like other men,
   In party colours strange to see;
The right side cloth of gold,
The left side to behold,
   Of woollen cloth still framèd he.
Men thereat did wonder,
Golden fame did thunder
   This strange deed in every place.
The king he coming thither,
Being pleasant weather,
   In the woods the hart to chase;
The children there did stand,
   As their mother willèd,
Where the royal king
   Must of force come by.
Their mother richly clad
   In fair crimson velvet;
Their father all in gray,

Most comely to the eye.
When this famous king,
Noting every thing,
　　Did ask him how he durst be so bold,
To let his wife to wear,
And deck his children there,
　　In costly robes of pearl and gold?
The forester bold replièd,
And the cause descrièd,
　　And to the king he thus did say:
Well may they by their mother,
Wear rich gold like other,
　　Being by birth a princess gay.
The king upon these words,
　　More heedfully beheld them;
Till a crimson blush
　　His conceit did cross.
The more I look, quoth he,
　　Upon thy wife and children,
The more I call to mind
　　My daughter whom I lost.
I am that child, quoth she,
Falling on her knee;
　　Pardon me, my soveraign liege.
The king perceiving this,
His daughter dear did kiss,
　　Till joyful tears did stop his speech.
With his train he turnèd,
And with her sojournèd;
　　Straight he dubb'd her husband knight;

He made him earl of Flanders,
One of his chief commanders;
Thus was their sorrow put to flight.

———

### XIV.

## THE FAITHFUL FRIENDSHIP OF TWO FRIENDS,

### ALPHONSO AND GANSELO.

To the Tune of " *Flying Fame*".

In stately Rome sometime did dwell
A man of noble fame,
Who had a son of seemly shape,
Alphonso was his name.

When he was grown and come to age,
His father thought it best
To send his son to Athens fair,
Where wisdom's school did rest.

And when he was to Athens come,
Good lectures for to learn,
A place to board him with delight,
His friends did well discern.

A noble knight of Athens town,
Of him did take the charge;
Who had a son, Ganselo call'd,
Just of his pitch and age;

In stature and in person both,
   In favour, speech, and face,
In quality and conditions eke,
   They 'greed in every place.

So like they were, in all respects,
   The one unto the other,
They were not known, but by their names,
   Of father or of mother.

And as in favour they were found
   Alike in all respects,
Even so they did most dearly love,
   As prov'd by good effects.

Ganselo lov'd a lady fair,
   Which did in Athens dwell,
Who was in beauty peerless found,
   So far she did excel.

Upon a time it chancèd so,
   As fancy did him move,
That he would visit, for delight,
   His lady and his loye;

And to his true and faithful friend,
   He declared the same;
Asking of him if he would see
   That fair and comely dame.

Alphonso did thereto agree;
  And with Ganselo went
To see the lady which he lov'd,
  Which bred his discontent.

But when he cast his crystal eyes
  Upon her angel's hue,
The beauty of that lady bright,
  Did straight his heart subdue,

His gentle heart so wounded was,
  With that fair lady's face,
That afterwards, he daily liv'd
  In sad and woful case;

And of his grief he knew not how
  Therefore to make an end;
For that he knew the lady's love,
  Was yielded to his friend.

Then being sore perplext in mind,
  Upon his bed he lay,
Like one which death and deep despair
  Had almost worn away.

His friend Ganselo that did see
  His grief and great distress,
At length requested for to know
  His cause of heaviness.

With much ado, at length he told
   The truth unto his friend;
Who did relieve his inward woe,
   With comfort to the end.

Take courage then, dear friend, quoth he,
   Though she through love be mine,
My right I will resign to thee;
   The lady shall be thine.

You know our favours are alike,
   Our speech also likewise;
This day in mine apparel
   You shall yourself disguise;

And unto church then shall you go,
   Directly in my stead;
Lo! though my friends suppose 'tis I,
   You shall the lady wed.

Alphonso was so well appaid,
   And as they had decreed,
He went that day and wedded plain
   The lady there indeed.

But when the nuptial-feast was done,
   And Phœbus quite was fled,
The lady for Ganselo took
   Alphonso to her bed.

That night was spent in pleasant sport,
 And when the day was come,
A post for fair Alphonso came,
 To fetch him home from Rome.

Then was the matter plainly proved,
 Alphonso wedded was,
And not Ganselo, to that dame,
 Which brought great woe, alas!

Alphonso being gone to Rome,
 With this his lady gay,
Ganselo's friends and kindred all,
 In such a rage did stay,

That they depriv'd him of his wealth,
 His land and rich attire,
And banish'd him their country quite,
 In rage and wrathful ire.

With sad and pensive thoughts, alas!
 Ganselo wandred then;
Who was constrain'd, thro' want, to beg
 Relief of many men.

In this distress oft would he say,
 To Rome I mean to go,
To seek Alphonso, my dear friend,
 Who will relieve my woe.

To Rome, when poor Ganselo came,
　And found Alphonso's place,
Which was so famous, huge, and fair,
　Himself in such poor case,

He was asham'd to shew himself
　In that his poor array;
Saying, Alphonso knows me well,
　If he would come this way :

Therefore he staid within the street;
　Alphonso then came by,
But heeding not Ganselo poor,
　His friend that stood so nigh ;

Which griev'd Ganselo to the heart.
　Quoth he, and is it so?
Doth proud Alphonso now disdain
　His friend indeed to know?

In desperate sort away he went,
　Into a barn hard by,
And presently he drew his knife,
　Thinking thereby to die.

And bitterly in sorrow there,
　Did he lament and weep :
And being over-weigh'd with grief,
　He there fell fast asleep.

F

While soundly there he sweetly slept,
  Came in a murthering thief,
And saw a naked knife lie by
  This man so full of grief.

The knife so bright he took up strait,
  And went away amain,
And thrust it in a murthered man,
  Which he before had slain;

And afterwards he went with speed,
  And put this bloody knife
Into his hand that sleeping lay,
  To save himself from strife.

Which done, away in haste he ran;
  And when that search was made,
Ganselo, with his bloody knife,
  Was for the murther staid,

And brought before the magistrate
  Who did confess most plain,
That he indeed, with that same knife,
  The murther'd man had slain.

Alphonso sitting then as judge,
  And knowing Ganselo's face,
To save his friend, did say himself
  Was guilty in that case.

None, quoth Alphonso, kill'd the man,
  My lord, but only I;
And, therefore, set this poor man free,
  And let me justly die.

Thus while for death these faithful friends
  In striving did proceed,
The man before the senate came,
  That did the fact indeed.

Who being movèd with remorse,
  Their friendly hearts to see,
Did say before the judges plain,
  None did the fact but he.

Thus when the truth was plainly told,
  Of all sides joy was seen;
Alphonso did embrace his friend,
  Which had so woful been.

In rich array he cloathèd him,
  As fitted his degree,
And helpt him to his lands again,
  And former dignity.

The murtherer, for telling truth,
  Had pardon at that time;
Who afterwards lamented much,
  His foul and grievous crime.

# THE SECOND PART.

### I.

### A PASTORAL SONG.

To the Tune of " *Hey ho holiday*," &c.

Upon a down, where shepherds keep,
  Piping pleasant lays,
Two country maids were keeping sheep,
  And sweetly chanted roundelays.

Three shepherds, each an oaten reed,
  Blaming Cupid's cruel wrong,
Unto these rural nymphs agreed
  To keep a tuneful under-song.

And so they were in number five,
  Musick's number sweet,
And we the like let us contrive,
  To sing their songs in order meet.

Fair Phillis's part I take to me,
  She 'gainst loving hinds complains ;
And Amarillis thou shalt be,
  She defends the shepherd swains.

*Ph.* Fie on the slights that men devise.

*Sh.*   Hey ho! silly slights.

*P.* When simple maids they would entice.

*S.*    Maidens are young men's chief delights.


*A.* Nay, women they with their eyes,

*S.*    Eyes like beams of charming sun.

*A.* And men once caught, they soon despise.

*S.*    So are shepherds oft undone.


*P.* If any young man win a maid.

*S.*    Happy man is he.

*P.* By trusting him she is betray'd.

*S.*    Fie upon such treachery!


*A.* If maids catch young men with their guiles.

*S.*    Hey ho! hey ho! guiltless grief.

*A.* They deal like weeping crocodiles.

*S.*    That murther man without relief.


*P.* I know a silly country hind.

*S.*    Hey ho! hey ho! silly swain!

*P.* To whom fair Daphne proved kind.

*S.*    Was he not kind to her again?


*P.* He vow'd to Pan with many an oath.

*S.*    Hey ho! hey ho! shepherds' god is he.

*A.* Yet since he hath chang'd, and broke his troth.

*S.*    Troth-plight broke, will plaguèd be.

*A.* She had deceivèd many a swain.

*S.*    Fie upon false deceit!

*A.* And plighted troth to them in vain.

*S.*    There can be no grief more great.


*A.* Her measure was with measure paid.

*S.*    Hey ho! hey ho! equal need.

*A.* She was beguil'd that was betray'd.

*S.*    So shall all deceivers speed.


*P.* If every maid were like to me.

*S.*    Hey ho! hey ho! hard of heart.

*P.* Both love and lovers scorn'd should be.

*S.*    Scorners should be sure of smart.


*A.* If every maid were of my mind.

*S.*    Hey ho! hey ho! lovely sweet.

*A.* They to their lovers should prove kind.

*S.*    Kindness is for maidens meet.


*P.* Methinks love is an idle toy.

*S.*    Hey ho! hey ho! busie pain.

*P.* Both wit and sense it doth annoy.

*S.*    Both wit and sense thereby we gain.


*A.* Tush! Philis, cease; be not so coy.

*P.*    Hey ho! hey ho! my disdain.

*A.* I know you love a shepherd's boy.

*S.*    Fie on that woman so can feign!

*P.* Well; Amarillis, now I yield.

*S.*     Shepherds sweetly pipe aloud.

*P.* Love conquers both in town and field.

*S.*     Like a tyrant, fierce and proud.

*A.* The evening-star is up we see.

*S.*     Vesper shines, we must away.

*P.* Would every lady would agree.

*S.*     So we end our roundelay.

———

II.

\*₊\* THE SINNER'S REDEMPTION: THE NATIVITY OF
OUR LORD & SAVIOUR JESUS CHRIST, WITH
HIS LIFE ON EARTH, AND PRECIOUS
DEATH ON THE CROSS.

ALL you that are to mirth inclin'd,
Consider well, and bear in mind
What our good God for us hath done,
In sending his belovèd son.

Let all our songs and praises be
Unto His heavenly majesty;
And evermore amongst our mirth,
Remember Christ our Saviour's birth.

The five and twentieth of December,
Good cause we have for to remember;
In Bethlehem, upon this morn,
There was our blest Messias born.

The night before that happy tide,
The spotless Virgin and her guide
Were long time seeking up and down,
To find them lodging in the town.

And mark how all things came to pass;
The inns and lodgings so fill'd was,
That they could have no room at all,
But in a silly ox's stall.

This night the Virgin Mary mild,
Was safe deliver'd of a child;
According unto heaven's decree,
Man's sweet salvation for to be.

Near Bethlehem did shepherds keep
Their herds and flocks of feeding sheep;
To whom God's angel did appear,
Which put the shepherds in great fear.

Prepare, and go, the angel said,
To Bethlehem! be not afraid;
There shall you see this blessèd morn,
The princely babe, sweet Jesus, born.

With thankful hearts, and joyful mind,
The shepherds went this babe to find;
And as the heavenly angel told,
They did our Saviour Christ behold.

Within a manger was he laid,
The Virgin Mary by him staid,
Attending on the Lord of life,
Being both mother, maid, and wife.

Three eastern wise men from afar,
Directed by a glorious star,
Came boldly on, and made no stay
Until they came where Jesus lay:

And being come unto the place
Wherein the blest Messias was,
They humbly laid before his feet,
Their gifts of gold and odours sweet.

See how the Lord of heaven and earth,
Shew'd himself lowly in his birth;
A sweet example for mankind
To learn to bear an humble mind.

No costly robes, nor rich attire,
Did Jesus Christ our Lord desire;
No musick, nor sweet harmony,
Till glorious angels from on high,

Did in melodious manner sing
Praises unto our heavenly king;
All honour, glory, might, and power,
Be unto Christ our Saviour.

If choirs of angels did rejoyce,
Well may mankind with heart and voice
Sing praises to the God of heaven,
That unto us a son hath given.

Moreover, let us every one
Call unto mind, and think upon
His righteous life, and how he dy'd
To have poor sinners justified.

Suppose, O! man, that thou shouldst lie
In prison strong, condemn'd to die,
And that no friend upon the earth
Could ransom thee from cruel death,

Except you can some party find,
That for your sake will be so kind,
His own heart's blood for to dispense,
And lose his life in thy defence.

Such was the love of Christ, when we
Were lost in hell perpetually,
To save us from the gulph of woe,
Himself much pain did undergo.

Whilst in this world he did remain,
He never spent one hour in vain;
In fasting, and in prayer divine,
He daily spent away the time;

He in the temple daily taught,
And many wonders strange he wrought.
He gave the blind their perfect sight,
And made the lame to walk upright:

He cur'd the lepers of their evils,
And by his power he cast out devils.
He raisèd Lazarus from the grave,
And to the sick their health he gave.

But yet for all these wonders wrought,
The Jews his dire destruction sought.
The traytor Judas was the man
That with a kiss betray'd him than.

Then was he led to Justice-hall,
Like one despis'd amongst them all;
And had the sentence given, that he
Should suffer death upon a tree.

Unto the execution-place
They brought him on with much disgrace;
With vile reproachful taunts and scorns,
They crown'd him with a wreath of thorns.

Then to the cross, through hands and feet,
They nail'd our blest Redeemer sweet;
And further to augment his smart,
With bloody spear they pierc'd his heart.

Thus have you seen and heard aright,
The love of Christ, the Lord of might;
And how He shed his precious blood,
Only to do us sinners good.

----

III.

\*.\* A WONDERFUL PROPHESIE, DECLARED BY CHRIS-
TIAN JAMES, A MAID OF TWENTY YEARS OF
AGE, WHO WAS BORN NEAR PADSTOW,
IN THE COUNTY OF CORNWAL, &c.

To the Tune of "*In Summer Time.*"

THE mighty Lord that rules in heaven,
   Strange wonders doth in England send;
And many warnings hath us given,
   'Cause we our lives should soon amend.

But like the misbelieving Jews,
   So hard of heart our people be,
They think that nothing can be true
   But that which their own eyes do see.

Therefore, good people, mark it well;
   I'll here lay open to your view
A song most wonderful and strange,
   And can approve it to be true.

A damsel did near Padstow dwell,
   Within the county of Cornwal fair,
Whose parents had no child but her;
   She was her father's only heir:

To whom came many a brave young man,
   Intending to make her a wife;
But never tempting tongue could make
   This damsel change her maiden life.

And though her parents riches had,
   And costly garments her allow'd;
In homely habit she would go,
   And alway hated to be proud.

She ne'er was heard to curse or swear,
   Nor any word of anger give;
But courteous was in every thing
   To them that did about her live.

If she heard any one to swear,
   Or take God's sacred name in vain,
She told them that they crucified
   Our Saviour Jesus Christ again.

She often did frequent the church,
  And also did relieve the poor;
The widow and the fatherless
  She every day fed at her door.

Upon a time this damsel she
  Fell sick, and in a deadly swound
She lay for twenty hours' space,
  No life in her then could be found.

Her aged father did lament,
  Her mother she shed many a tear;
She wept, she wail'd, she wrung her hands,
  For loss of this her daughter dear.

Alas! alas! my child, she said,
  How dearly have I tendered thee,
And wilt thou now forsake the world
  And leave me in this misery?

I would thy birth had been my death,
  Then never had I known this day.
This grievous moan her mother made
  By her dear daughter as she lay.

At last she did strong waters fetch,
  And rubb'd her temples and each vein,
Till at the last the damsel had
  Recover'd life and sense again.

And being come unto her speech,
  With voice most shrill, aloud she cried,
O, mother, you have done me wrong,
  This cannot be by you denied.

For I was in the way to heaven,
  Two glorious angels did me guide,
Who gently took me by the hand,
  And helped me up on every side;

Singing of psalms and spiritual songs,
  So long as we pass'd on the way;
Till he which had a golden crown
  Met us, and causèd us to stay.

Return, said he, from whence thou cam'st,
  Thy mother for thee makes great moan;
And tell these things, which I declare,
  Unto thy neighbours every one.

Speak this, quoth he, unto them all;
  How that the Lord, e'er long, will send
A grievous punishment to them
  That wilfully his will offend.

This is the last age of the world,
  Even to the very sink of sin,
The puddle of iniquity
  Which you long time have wallowed in.

The men and wives live in discord ;
  The father envies his own son ;
The rich, the poor, the old, the young,
  Do hourly into mischief run.

Extortion and idolatry,
  And hateful pride are now in use ;
Blasphemous oaths, and curses vile,
  The people count as no abuse.

Good ministers are set at nought,
  The Sabbath is profan'd also ;
The poor lie starving in the street,
  Opprest with sorrow, grief and woe.

The loathsome sin of drunkenness
  And whoredom, doth too much exceed ;
He that can do his neighbour wrong,
  Doth think he doth a goodly deed.

Now ponder well what I do say ;
  Doom's dreadful day is nigh at hand ;
Fire and brimstone shall destroy
  The heaven, the earth, the sea and land:

And every soul before the Lord
  A just account he then shall give ;
His conscience shall a witness be,
  In what condition he did live.

Then he that hath done well shall pass
Forthwith to everlasting rest,
And live among those glorious saints
Which Jesus Christ our Lord hath blest.

Where martyrs, prophets, and patriarchs,
Do hallelujahs ever sing;
Glory and honour be to God,
And unto Christ our heavenly king.

Then woe to them that have done ill,
When they shall hear the sentence past,
Depart ye cursed into hell,
Whose fire for evermore shall last.

The sorrows which are here foretold
Will come on you, e'er it be long;
Except repentance truly dwell
In hearts of all, both old and young.

Repentance, and true wat'ry eyes,
Will help to quench the burning flame,
Which he hath kindled to consume
This wicked world's most rotten frame.

Let not your building, all so brave,
Be burnt and wasted with God's ire;
Nor let your souls, for whom Christ died,
Be burnt in hell's eternal fire.

*Here endeth the Prophesie.*

These speeches spoke, the maiden died,
   And came no more to life again;
Her soul, no doubt, is gone to heaven,
   With glorious angels to remain.

At her decease, an harmony
   Of musick there was heard to sound,
Which ravish'd all the standers-by,
   It did with sweetness so abound;

It pierc'd the earth and air also,
   Yet no man knew from whence it came;
But each one said it came from heaven;
   And presently, upon the same,

The magistrates of that same parish,
   Which heard and saw this wonder strange,
Desir'd to have it put in print,
   'Cause wicked men their ways may change.

---

IV.

OF PATIENT GRISSEL AND A NOBLE MARQUESS.

To the Tune of "*The Bride's Good-morrow.*"

A NOBLE marquess, as he did ride a-hunting,
   Hard by a river side,
A proper maiden, as she did sit a-spinning,
   His gentle eye espy'd:

Most fair and lovely, and of comely grace was she,
  Although in simple attire;
She sang most sweetly, with pleasant voice melodiously,
  Which set the Lord's heart on fire.
The more he lookt, the more he might,
Beauty bred, his heart's delight;
  And to this damsel he went.
God speed, quoth he, thou famous flower,
Fair mistress of this homely bower,
Where love and vertue live with sweet content.

With comely gesture, and modest mild behaviour,
  She bad him welcome then;
She entertain'd him in a friendly manner,
  And all his gentlemen.
The noble marquess in his heart felt such flame,
  Which set his senses all at strife.
Quoth he, fair maiden, shew soon what is thy name?
  I mean to take thee to my wife.
Grissel is my name, quoth she,
Far unfit for your degree;
  A silly maiden, and of parents poor.
Nay, Grissel, thou art rich, he said,
A vertuous, fair, and comely maid;
  Grant me thy love, and I will ask no more.

At length she consented, and being both contented,
  They married were with speed:
Her country russet was turn'd to silk and velvet,
  As to her state agreed:

And when that she was trimly attirèd in the same,
 Her beauty shin'd most bright;
Far staining every other brave and comely dame
 That did appear in her sight.
Many envied her therefore,
Because she was of parents poor,
 And 'twixt her lord and her great strife did raise:
Some said this, and some said that;
Some did call her beggar's brat;
 And to her lord they would her oft dispraise.


O, noble marquess, quoth they, why do you wrong us,
 Thus basely for to wed;
That might have got an honourable lady
 Into your princely bed?
Who will not now your noble issue still deride,
 Which shall be hereafter born,
That are of blood so base by the mother's side,
 The which will bring them to scorn?
Put her, therefore, quite away;
Take to you a lady gay,
 Whereby your lineage may renownèd be.
Thus every day they seem'd to prate
At malic'd Grissel's good estate,
 Who took all this most mild and patiently.


When that the marquess did see that they were bent thus
 Against his faithful wife,
Whom most dearly, tenderly, and intirely,
 He lovèd as his l'fe:

Minding in secret for to prove her patient heart,
   Thereby her foes to disgrace;
Thinking to play a hard discourteous part,
   That men might pity her case.
Great with child this lady was,
And at length it came to pass,
   Two lovely children at one birth she had;
A son and daughter God had sent,
Which did their father well content,
   And which did make their mother's heart full glad.

Great royal feasting was at the children's christ'ning,
   And princely triumph made
Six weeks together, all nobles that came thither,
   Were entertain'd and staid.
And when that these pleasant sportings quite were done,
   The marquess a messenger sent
For his young daughter and his pretty smiling son;
   Declaring his full intent,
How that the babes must murthered be,
For so the marquess did decree.
   Come, let me have the children, he said.
With that fair Grissel wept full sore,
She wrung her hands and said no more,
   My gracious lord must have his will obey'd.

She took the babies from the nursing-ladies,
   Between her tender arms;
She often wishes, with many sorrowful kisses,
   That she might help their harms.

Farewel, quoth she, my children dear,
  Never shall I see you again;
'Tis long of me, your sad and woful mother dear,
  For whose sake you must be slain:
Had I been born of royal race,
You might have liv'd in happy case;
  But now you must die for my unworthiness.
Come, messenger of death, quoth she,
Take my despisèd babes to thee,
  And to their father my complaints express.

He took the children, and to his noble master
  He brought them forth with speed;
Who secretly sent them unto a noble lady
  To be nurst up indeed.
Then to fair Grissel with a heavy heart he goes,
  Where she sat mildly all alone,
A pleasant gesture and a lovely look she shows,
  As if grief she had never known.
Quoth he, my children now are slain;
What thinks fair Grissel of the same?
  Sweet Grissel, now declare thy mind to me.
Since you, my lord, are pleas'd with it,
Poor Grissel thinks the action fit;
  Both I and mine at your command will be.

The nobles murmur, fair Grissel, at thine honour,
  And I no joy can have
'Till thou be banisht from my court and presence.
  As they unjustly crave.

Thou must be stript out of thy stately garments;
  And as thou camest to me,
In homely gray, instead of silk and purest pall,
  Now all thy cloathing must be;
My lady thou must be no more,
Nor I thy lord, which grieves me sore;
  The poorest life must now content thy mind:
A groat to thee I may not give,
Thee to maintain while I do live;
  'Gainst my Grissel such great foes I find.

When gentle Grissel heard these woful tidings,
  The tears stood in her eyes;
She nothing said; no words of discontentment
  Did from her lips arise:
Her velvet gown most patiently she stript off,
  Her girdle of silk with the same:
Her russet gown was brought again with many a scoff;
  To bear them all, herself did frame:
When she was drest in this array,
And ready was to part away,
  God send long life unto my lord, quoth she;
Let no offence be found in this
To give my lord a parting kiss.
  With wat'ry eyes, Farewel! my dear, quoth he.

From stately palace, unto her father's cottage,
  Poor Grissel now is gone;
Full fifteen winters she lived there contented,
  No wrong she thought upon;

And at that time thro' all the land the speeches went,
  The marquess should married be
Unto a noble lady of high descent,
  And to the same all parties did agree.
The marquess sent for Grissel fair,
The bride's bed-chamber to prepare,
  That nothing should therein be found awry;
The bride was with her brother come,
Which was great joy to all and some;
  And Grissel took all this most patiently.

And in the morning when that they should be wedded,
  Her patience now was try'd;
Grissel was chargèd in princely manner
  For to attire the bride.
Most willingly she gave consent unto the same;
  The bride in her bravery was drest,
And presently the noble marquess thither came,
  With all the ladies at his request.
Oh! Grissel, I would ask of thee
If to this match thou wouldst agree?
  Methinks thy looks are waxèd wond'rous coy.
With that they all began to smile,
And Grissel she replies the while,
  God send lord marquess many years of joy!

The marquis was movèd to see his best belovèd
  Thus patient in distress;
He stept unto her, and by the hand he took her,
  These words he did express;

Thou art the bride, and all the brides I mean to have;
  These two thy own children be.
The youthful lady on her knees did blessing crave,
  The brother as willing as she:
And you that envy her estate,
Whom I have made my loving mate,
  Now blush for shame, and honour vertuous life;
The chronicles of lasting fame,
Shall evermore extol the name
  Of patient Grissel, my most constant wife.

---

v.

## A PLEASANT SONG BETWEEN PLAIN TRUTH, AND BLIND IGNORANCE.

*Truth.*   God speed you, ancient father,
     And give you a good daye:
    What is the cause, I praye you,
     So sadly here you staye?
    And that you keep such gazing
     On this decayèd place,
    The which, for superstition,
     Good princes down did raze?

*Ign.*   Chill tell thee by my vazen,
     That zometimes che have knowne;
    A vair and goodly abbey,
     Stand here of bricke and stone:

And many a holy vrier,
　　As ich may say to thee,
Within these goodly cloysters,
　　Che did full often zee.


*Truth.*　Then I must tell thee, father,
　　In truth and veritie,
A sorte of greater hypocrites,
　　Thou couldst not likely see :
Deceiving of the simple,
　　With false and feignèd lies ;
But such an order, truly,
　　Christ never did devise.


*Ign.*　Ah ! ah ! che zmell thee now, man ;
　　Che know well what thou art ;
A vellow of mean learning,
　　Che was not worth a vart :
Vor when we had the old lawe,
　　A merry world was then,
And every thing was plenty
　　Among all zortes of men.


*Truth.*　Thou givest me an answer,
　　As did the Jews sometimes
Unto the prophet Jeremye,
　　When he accus'd their crimes.
'Twas merry, said the people,
　　And joyful in our rea'me,
Which did offer spice-cakes
　　Unto the queen of heav'n.

*Iyn.*   Chill tell thee what, good vellowe;
    Bevore the vicars went hence,
  A bushel of the best wheate
    Was zold for vourteen pence,
  And vorty egges a penny,
    That were both good and newe;
  And this zhe zay my zelf have zeene,
    And yet ich am no Jewe.

*Truth.*   Within the sacred bible,
    We find it written plaine,
  The latter days should troublesome
    And dangerous be, certaine;
  That we should be self-lovers,
    And charity wax colde;
  Then 'tis not true religion
    That makes thee grief to holde.

*Iyn.*   Chill tell thee my opinion plaine,
    And choul that well ye knewe;
  Ich care not for the bible booke,
    'Tis too big to be true:
  Our blessed ladye's psalter,
    Zhall for my money goe;
  Zuch pretty prayers as there bee,
    The bible cannot zhowe.

*Truth.*   Now thou hast spoken trulye;
    For in that book, indeede,
  No mention of our ladye,
    Or Romish saint we reade:

For by the blessed Spirit
　　That book indited was,
And not by simple persons,
　　As is the foolish masse.


*Ign.*　　Cham zure they are not voolishe
　　　　That made the masse, che trowe;
　　Why, man, 'tis all in Latine,
　　　　And vools no Latine knowe:
　　Were not our fathers wise men,
　　　　And they did like it well?
　　Who very much rejoycèd
　　　　To hear the zeering bell?


*Truth.*　　But many kings and prophets,
　　　　As I may say to thee,
　　Have wisht the light that you have,
　　　　And could it never see;
　　For what art thou the better,
　　　　A Latine song to hear,
　　And understandeth nothing
　　　　That they sing in the quiere?


*Ign.*　　O! hold thy peace, che pray thee,
　　　　The noise was passing trim,
　　To hear the vriers zinging,
　　　　As we did enter in:
　　And then to zee the rood-loft
　　　　Zo bravely zet with zaints,
　　And now to zee them wand'ring,
　　　　My heart with zorrow vaints.

*Truth.*　The Lord did give commandment,
　　　　No image thou shouldst make,
　　　　Nor that unto idolatry
　　　　　You should yourself betake :
　　　　The golden calf of Israel
　　　　　Moses did therefore spoile,
　　　　And Baal's priests and temple
　　　　　He brought to utter foile.

*Ign.*　But our ladye of Walsinghame
　　　　Was a pure and holy zaint,
　　　　And many men in pilgrimage,
　　　　　Did zhew to her complaint :
　　　　Yea, with zweet Thomas Becket,
　　　　　And many other moe,
　　　　The holy maid of Kent, likewise,
　　　　　Did many wonders zhowe.

*Truth.*　Such saints are well agreeing
　　　　To your profession sure ;
　　　　And to the men that made them
　　　　　So precious and so pure :
　　　　The one was found a traytoure,
　　　　　And judg'd worthy of death ;
　　　　The other eke for treason
　　　　　Did end his hateful breath.

*Ign.*　Yea, yea, it is no matter,
　　　　Dispraise them as you wille ;
　　　　But zure they did much goodnesse,
　　　　　Would they were with us stille !

We had our holy water,
  And holy bread likewise;
And many holy reliques
  We zaw before our eyes.

*ruth.*  And all this while they fed you
  With vain and sundry shows,
Which never Christ commanded,
  As learnèd doctor knows;
Search then the holy scriptures,
  And thou shalt plainly see,
That headlong to damnation
  They alway trainèd thee.

*n.*  If it be true, good vellowe,
  As thou dost zay to mee,
Then to my zaviour Jesus,
  Alone then will Ich flee;
Believing in the gospel,
  And passion of his Zon,
And with the zubtil papistes
  Ich have for ever done.

————————

## VI

## THE OVERTHROW OF PROUD HOLOFORNES, AND
## THE TRIUMPH OF VERTUOUS QUEEN JUDETH.

WHEN king Nebuchadnezzar
  Was puffèd up with pride,
He sent forth many men of war,
  By Holofornes guide,
To plague and spoil the world throughout,
  By fierce Bellona's rod.
That would not fear and honour him,
  And acknowledge him their god.

Which when the holy Israelites
  Did truly understand,
For to prevent this tyranny
  They fortified their land;
Their towns and stately cities strong
  They did with victuals store;
Their warlike weapons they prepar'd,
  Their furious foe to gore.

When stately Holofornes then
  Had knowledge of that thing,
That they had thus prepar'd themselves
  For to withstand the king,

Quoth he, what god is able now
  To keep these men from me?
Is there a greater than our king,
  Whom all men fear to see?

Come, march with me, therefore, he said,
  My captains every one,
And first unto Bethulia
  With speed let us be gone;
I will destroy each mother's son
  That is within the land;
Their God shall not deliver them
  Out of my furious hand.

Wherefore about Bethulia,
  That little city then,
On foot he planted up and down,
  An hundred thousand men;
Twelve thousand more, on horses brave,
  About the town had he;
He stopt their springs and water-pipes
  To work their misery.

When four and thirty days they had
  With wars besiegèd been,
The poor Bethulians at that time,
  So thirsty then were seen,
That they were like to starve and dye,
  They were both weak and faint;
The people 'gainst the rulers cry,
  And this was their complaint:

Better it is for us, quoth they,
  To yield unto our foe,
Than by this great and grievous thirst,
  To be destroyèd so :
O ! render up the town, therefore,
  We are forsaken quite ;
There is no means to escape their hands,
  Who might escape their might ?

Whenas their grievèd rulers heard
  The clamours which they made,
Good people, be content, said they,
  And be no whit dismay'd ;
Yet five days stay in hope of health,
  God will reward your woe ;
But if by then no succour come,
  We'll yield unto our foe.

When Judeth, prudent, princely dame,
  Had tydings of this thing,
Which was Manesses' beauteous wife,
  That sometime was their king,
Why tempt ye God so sore, she said,
  Before all men this day,
Whom mortal men in conscience ought
  To fear and eke obey ?

If you will grant me leave, quoth she,
  To pass abroad this night,
To Holofornes I will go,
  For all his furious might ;                    H

But what I do intend to do,
  Enquire not now of me.
Go then in peace, fair dame, they said,
  And God be still with thee.

When she from them was gotten home,
  Within her palace-gate,
She callèd to her chiefest maid,
  That on her then did wait;
Bring me my best attire, quoth she,
  And jewels of fine gold;
And wash me with the finest balms
  That are for silver sold.

The fairest, and the richest robe
  That then she did possess,
Upon her dainty corpse she put;
  And eke her hair did dress
With costly pearls, and precious stones,
  And earrings of fine gold;
That like an angel she did seem,
  Most sweet for to behold.

A pot of sweet and pleasant oil
  She took with her that time,
A bag of figs, and fine wheat-flower,
  A bottle of fine wine,
Because she would not eat with them
  That worship gods of stone:
And from her city thus she went,
  With one poor maid alone.

Much ground, alas! she had not gone,
  Out of her own city,
But that the centinels espy'd
  A woman wond'rous pritty;
From whence came you, fair maid? quoth they,
  And where walk you so late?
From yonder town, good sirs, quoth she,
  To your lord of high estate.

When they did mark and view her well,
  And saw her fair beauty,
And therewithal her rich array,
  So gorgeous to the eye,
They were amazèd in their minds,
  So fair a dame to see!
They set her in a chariot then,
  In place of high degree.

An hundred proper chosen men,
  They did appoint likewise,
To wait on princely Judeth there,
  Whose beauty clear'd their eyes:
And all the soldiers running came
  To view her as she went;
And thus with her they past along,
  Unto the general's tent.

Then came his stately guard in haste,
  Fair Judeth for to meet,
And to their high, renownèd lord,
  They brought this lady sweet:    H 2

And then before his honour there,
 Upon her knee she fell;
Her beauty bright made him to muse,
 So far she did excell.

Rise up, renownèd dame, quoth he,
 The glory of thy kind,
And be no whit amaz'd at all,
 To shew to me thy mind!
When she had utter'd her intent,
 Her wit amaz'd them all;
And Holofornes therewith he
 By love was brought to thrall.

And bearing in his lofty breast
 The flames of hot desire,
He granted every thing to her
 She did of him require;
Each night, therefore, he gave her leave
 To walk abroad to pray,
According to her own request,
 Which she had made that day.

When she in camp had three days been,
 Near Holofornes' tent,
His chiefest friend, lord treasurer,
 Unto her then he sent;
Fair dame, quoth he, my lord commands
 This night your company;
Quoth she, I will not my dear lord
 In any thing deny.

A very great and sumptuous feast
   Did Holofornes make
Amongst the [warlike] lords and knights,
   And all for Judeth's sake;
But of their dainties, in no case
   Would pleasant Judeth taste,
Yet Holofornes merry was,
   So near him she was plac'd.

And being very pleasantly
   Disposèd at that time,
He drunk with them abundantly
   Of strong delicious wine;
So that his strength and memory,
   So far from him were fled,
They laid him down, and Judeth then
   Was brought unto his bed.

When all the doors about were shut,
   And every one was gone,
Hard by the pillow of his bed,
   His sword she 'spy'd anon;
Then down she took it presently;
   To God for strength she pray'd;
She cut his head from shoulders quite,
   And gave it to her maid.

The rich and golden canopy
   That hung over his bed,
She took the same with her likewise,
   With Holofornes' head;

And thus through all the court of guards,
　　She escapèd clean away;
None did her stay, thinking that she
　　Had gone forth for to pray.

When she had pass'd, escapèd quite
　　The danger of them all,
And that she was come near unto
　　The besiegèd city's wall,
Come open me the gates, quoth she,
　　Our foe the Lord hath slain;
See here his head within my hand,
　　That bore so great a fame.

Upon a pole they pitcht his head,
　　That all men might it 'spy,
And o'er the city wall forthwith,
　　They set it presently;
Then all the soldiers in the town
　　March'd forth in rich array;
But soon their foes 'spy'd their approach,
　　For 'twas at break of day.

Then running hastily to call
　　Their general out of bed,
They found his lifeless body there,
　　But clean without his head;
When this was known, all in amaze,
　　They fled away each man;
They left their tents full rich behind,
　　And so away they ran.

Lo! here behold how God provides
  For them that in him trust;
When earthly hopes are all in vain,
  He takes us from the dust!
How often hath our Judeth sav'd,
  And kept us from decay
'Gainst Holofornes and the pope,
  As may be seen this day?

---

VII.

## A PRINCELY DITTY, IN PRAISE OF THE
## ENGLISH ROSE.

Translated out of the French.

AMONGST the princely paragons,
Bedeckt with dainty diamonds,
Within mine eye, none doth come nigh
The sweet red Rose of England.
  The lilies pass in bravery,
  In Flanders, Spain, and Italy,
  But yet the famous flower of France
  Doth honour the Rose of England.

As I abroad was walking,
I heard the small birds talking;
And every one did frame her song
In praise of the Rose of England,
  The lilies, &c.

Cæsar may vaunt of victories,
And Crœsus of his happiness;
But he were blest, that may bear in his breast
The sweet red Rose of England.
  The lilies, &c.

The bravest lute bring hither,
And let us sing together,
Whilst I do ring, on every string,
The praise of the Rose of England.
  The lilies, &c.

The sweetest perfumes and spices
The wise men brought to Jesus,
Did never smell a quarter so well
As doth the Rose of England.
  The lilies, &c.

Then fair and princely flower,
That over my heart doth tower,
None may be compared to thee,
Which art the fair Rose of England.
  The lilies, &c.

### *⁎* A COMMUNICATION BETWEEN FANCY AND DESIRE.

COME hither, shepherd's swain.
   Sir, what do you require?
I pray thee shew thy name?
   My name is FOND DESIRE.

When wast thou born, Desire?
   In pomp and pride of May.
By whom, sweet child, wast thou begot?
   Of fond Conceit, men say.

Tell me who was thy nurse?
   Sweet Youth, and sug'red joys.
What was thy meat and dainty food?
   Sad sighs and great annoys.

What hadst thou for to drink?
   Unsavoury lovers tears.
What cradle wast thou rockèd in?
   In love, devoid of fears.

What lull'd thee then asleep?
   Sweet speech, which likes me best.
Tell me where is thy dwelling-place?
   In gentle hearts I rest.

What thing doth please thee most?
  To gaze on beauty still.
Whom dost thou think to be thy foe?
  Disdain of my good-will.

Doth company displease?
  Yea, sure, many one.
Where doth Desire delight to live?
  He loves to live alone.

Doth either time or age
  Bring him unto decay?
No, no; Desire both lives and dies
  Ten thousand times a day.

Then, fond Desire, farewel!
  Thou art no meat for me;
I should be lothe to dwell
  With such a one as thee.

THE END OF THE SECOND PART.

# THE THIRD PART.

I.

## A MAIDEN'S CHOICE 'TWIXT AGE AND YOUTH.

CRABBED age and youth
  Cannot live together;
Youth is full of pleasure,
  Age is full of care;
Youth 's like summer's morn,
  Age like winter's weather;
Youth is full of sport,
Agè's breath is short.

  Youth is wild, and age is lame;
Youth is hot and bold,
  Age is weak and cold;
  Youth is wild, and age is tame;
Age, I do abhor thee!
Youth, I do adore thee!
  O! my love, my lord is young;
Age, I do defie thee!
O! sweet shepherd, hye thee,
  For methinks thou stay'st too long.

Here I do attend,
  Arm'd by love and pleasure,
With my youthful friend
  Joyful for to meet :
Here I do await
  For my only treasure ;
Venus' sugar'd habit,
  Fancy's dainty sweet.


Like a loving wife,
So I lead my life,
  Thirsting for my heart's desire ;
Come, sweet youth, I pray,
Away, old man, away,
  Thou canst not give what I require ;
For old Age I care not ;
Come, my love, and spare not ;
  Age is feeble, Youth is strong ;
Age, I do defie thee !
O ! sweet shepherd, hye thee ;
  For methinks thou stay'st too long.


Phœbus, stay thy steeds,
  Over-swiftly running ;
Drive not on so fast
  Bright resplendent sun ;
For fair Daphne's sake,
  Now express thy cunning ;
Pity on me take
  Else I am undone ;

Your hours swift of flight,
That wake with Titan's sight,
  And so consume the chearful day;
O! stay a while with me,
Till I my love may see;
  O! Youth, thou dost so long delay:

Time will over-slip us,
And in pleasure trip us;
  Come away, therefore, with speed;
I would not lose an hour
For fair London's tower;
  Venus, therefore, help my need:
Flora's banks are spread
  In their rich attire,
With their dainty violet,
  And the primrose sweet
Daisies white and red,
  Fitting Youth's desire,
Whereby the daffidilly
  And the cowslip meet.

All for Youth's behove,
Their fresh colours move
  In the meadows green and gay;
The birds, with sweeter notes,
So strain their pretty throats
  To entertain my love this way;
I wish twenty wishes,
And an hundred kisses,

Would receive him by the hand;
If he give not me a fall,
I would him coward call,
    And all unto my wôrd would stand.

Lo! here he appears,
    Like to young Adonis,
Ready to set on fire
    The chastest heart alive;
Jewel of my life,
    Welcome where thine own is;
Pleasant are thy looks,
    Sorrows to deprive;
Embracing thy darling dear,
Without all doubtful fear.
    On thy command I wholly rest;
Do what thou wilt to me,
Therein I agree,
    And be not strange to my request;
To Youth I only yield;
Age fits not Venus' field,
    Though I be conquer'd, what care I?
In such a pleasant war,
Come meet me if you dare!
    Who first mislikes, let them cry.

II.

## AS I CAME FROM WALSINGHAM.

As you came from the holy-land
  Of Walsingham,
Met you not with my true love
  By the way as you came?

How should I know your true love,
  That have met many a one
As I came from the holy-land,
  That have come, that have gone?

She is neither white nor brown,
  But as the heavens fair;
There is none hath a form so divine,
  On the earth, in the air.

Such a one did I meet, (good sir)
  With angel like face;
Who like a queen did appear
  In her gait, in her grace.

She hath left me here all alone,
  All alone and unknown,
Who sometime lov'd me as her life,
  And call'd me her own.

What's the cause she hath left thee alone,
  And a new way doth take,

That sometime did love thee as her life,
    And her joy did thee make?

I lovèd her all my youth,
    But now am old, as you see;
Love liketh not the fallen fruit,
    Nor the witherèd tree:

For love is a careless child,
    And forgets promise past;
He is blind, he is deaf, when he list,
    And in faith never fast.

For love is a great delight,
    And yet a trustless joy;
He is won with a word of despair,
    And is lost with a toy.

Such is the love of womankind,
    Or the word (love) abus'd,
Under which many childish desires
    And conceits are excus'd.

But love is a durable fire,
    In the mind ever burning;
Never sick, never dead, never cold,
    From itself never turning.

III.

## AN EXCELLENT SONG ON THE WINNING OF CALES BY THE ENGLISH.

Long had the proud Spaniards
  Advancèd to conquer us,
Threatening our country
  With fire and sword;
Often preparing
  Their navy most sumptuous,
With all the provision
  That Spain could afford.
    Dub a-dub, dub,
      Thus strike the drums,
    Tan-ta-ra, ta-ra-ra,
      The English man comes.

To the seas presently
  Went our lord admiral,
With knights couragious,
  And captains full good;
The earl of Essex,
  A prosperous general,
With him preparèd
  To pass the salt flood.
    Dub a-dub, &c.

At Plymouth speedily,
  Took they ships valiantly;

I

Braver ships never
  Were seen under sail;
With their fair colours spread,
  And streamers o'er their head;
Now, bragging Spaniards,
  Take heed of your tail.
    Dub a-dub, &c.

Unto Cales cunningly,
  Came we most happily,
Where the kings navy
  Did secretly ride;
Being upon their backs,
  Piercing their buts of sack,
Ere that the Spaniards
  Our coming descry'd.
    Tan-ta-ra, ta-ra-ra,
      The English man comes;
    Bounce a-bounce, bounce a-bounce,
      Off went the guns.

Great was the crying,
  Running and riding,
Which at that season
  Was made at that place;
Then beacons were firèd,
  As need was requirèd;
To hide their great treasure,
  They had little space:
    Alas! they cryèd,
      English men comes.

There you might see the ships,
How they were firèd fast,
And how the men drown'd
Themselves in the sea;
There you may hear them cry,
Wail and weep piteously;
When as they saw no shift
To escape thence away.
Dub a-dub, &c.

The great *Saint Philip*,
The pride of the Spaniards,
Was burnt to the bottom,
And sunk in the sea;
But the *Saint Andrew*,
And eke the *Saint Matthew*,
We took in fight manfully,
And brought them away.
Dub a-dub, &c.

The earl of Essex,
Most valiant and hardy,
With horsemen and footmen
March'd towards the town;
The enemies which saw them,
Full greatly affrighted,
Did fly for their safeguard,
And durst not come down.
Dub a-dub, &c.

Now, quoth the noble earl,
　　Courage, my soldiers all!
Fight, and be valiant,
　　And spoil you shall have;
And well rewarded all,
　　From the great to the small;
But look that the women
　　And children you save.
　　　　Dub a-dub, &c.

The Spaniards at that sight,
　　Saw 'twas in vain to fight,
Hung up their flags of truce,
　　Yielding the town;
We march'd in presently,
　　Decking the walls on high
With our English colours,
　　Which purchas'd renown.
　　　　Dub a-dub, &c.

Ent'ring the houses then
　　And of the richest men,
For gold and treasure
　　We searchèd each day;
In some places we did find
　　Pye baking in the oven,
Meat at the fire roasting,
　　And men run away.
　　　　Dub a-dub, &c.

Full of rich merchandize,
   Every shop we did see,
Damask and sattins
   And velvet full fair ;
Which soldiers measure out
   By the length of their swords ;
Of all commodities,
   Each one hath share.
      Dub a-dub, &c.

Thus Cales was taken,
   And our brave general
March'd to the market-place,
   There he did stand ;
There many prisoners
   Of good account were took ;
Many crav'd mercy,
   And mercy they found.
      Dub a-dub, &c.

When as our general
   Saw they delayèd time,
And would not ransom
   The town as they said,
With their fair wainscots,
   Their presses and bedsteads,
Their joint-stools and tables,
   A fire we made :
And when the town burnt in a flame,
   With tan-ta-ra, tan-ta-ra-rara,
From thence we came.

IV.

### OF KING EDWARD THE THIRD, AND THE FAIR
### COUNTESS OF SALISBURY.

Setting forth her constancy and endless glory.

WHEN as Edward the third did live,
    That valiant king,
David of Scotland to rebel
    Did then begin ;
The town of Barwick suddenly
    From us he won,
And burnt Newcastle to the ground ;
    Thus strife begun :
To Roxbury castle marcht he then,
And by the force of warlike men,
    Besieg'd therein a gallant fair lady,
While that her husband was in France,
His country's honour to advance,
    The noble and famous earl of Salisbury.

Brave Sir William Montague
    Rode then in haste,
Who declarèd unto the king
    The Scottish men's boast ;
Who, like a lyon in his rage,
    Did straightway prepare
For to deliver that fair lady
    From woful care ;

But when the Scottish men did hear her say,
Edward our king was come that day,
   They rais'd their siege, and ran away with speed;
So when that he did thither come,
With warlike trumpet, fife and drum,
   None but a gallant lady did he meet indeed.

Whom when he did with greedy eyes
   Behold and see,
Her peerless beauty it inthrall'd
   His majesty;
And ever the longer that he lookt,
   The more he might;
For in her only beauty was
   His heart's delight:
And humbly then upon her knee,
She thank'd his royal majesty
   That he had driven danger from her gate.
Lady, quoth he, stand up in peace!
Although my war doth now increase.
   Lord keep, quoth she, all hurt from your estate.

Now is the king full sad in soul,
   And wots not why;
And for the love of the fair countess
   Of Salisbury;
She little knowing this cause of his grief,
   Did come to see
Wherefore his highness sate alone
   So heavily;

I have been wrong'd, fair dame, quoth he,
Since I came hither unto thee.
    No, God forbid! my sovereign, said she;
If I were worthy for to know
The cause and ground of this your woe,
    You should be helpt, if it did lie in me.


Swear to perform thy word to me,
    Thou lady gay,
To thee the sorrows of my heart
    I will bewray.
I swear by all the saints in heaven
    I will (quoth she);
And let my lord have no mistrust
    At all in me.
Then take thyself aside, he said;
For why, thy beauty hath betray'd;
    Wounding a king with thy bright shining eye
If thou do then some mercy show,
Thou shalt expel a princely woe;
    So shall I live, or else in sorrow die.


You have your wish, my soveraign lord,
    Effectually;
Take all the leave that I can give
    Your Majesty.
But on thy beauty all my joys
    Have their abode.
Take thou my beauty from my face,
    My gracious lord.

Didst thou not swear to grant my will?
That I may, I will fulfil.
   All then for my love, let my true love be seen.
My lord, your speech I might reprove;
You cannot give to me your love,
   For that belongs unto your queen.

But I suppose your grace did this
   Only to try
Whether a wanton tale might tempt
   Dame Salisbury;
Not from yourself, therefore, my liege,
   My steps do stray,
But from your wanton tempting tale,
   I go my way.
O! turn again, my lady bright;
Come unto me my heart's delight!
   Gone is the comfort of my pensive heart:
Here comes the earl of Warwick; he,
The father of this fair lady,
   My mind to him I mean for to impart.

Why is my lord and sovereign king
   So griev'd in mind?
Because that I have lost the thing
   I cannot find.
What thing is that, my gracious lord,
   Which you have lost?
It is my heart, which is near dead
   Betwixt fire and frost.

Curst be that fire and frost also,
That causèd this your Highness woe.
　　O! Warwick, thou dost wrong me very sore;
It is thy daughter, noble earl,
That heaven-bright lamp, that pearless pearl,
　　Which kills my heart, yet do I her adore.


If that be all, my gracious king,
　　That works your grief,
I will persuade the scornful dame
　　To yield relief;
Never shall she my daughter be
　　If she refuse;
The love and favour of a king
　　May her excuse.
Thus wise Warwick went away,
And quite contráry he did say
　　When as he did the beauteous countess meet.
Well met, my daughter, then quoth he,
A message I must do to thee;
　　Our royal king most kindly doth thee greet;


The king will die 'less thou to him
　　Do grant thy love.
To love the king, my husband's love
　　I would remove.
It is right charity to love,
　　My daughter dear,
But no true love so charitable
　　For to appear;

His greatness may bear out the shame,
But his kingdom cannot buy out the blame;
   He craves thy love, that may bereave thy life;
It is my duty to move this,
But not thy honesty to yield, I wis.
   I mean to die a true unspotted wife!

Now hast thou spoken, my daughter dear,
   As I would have;
Chastity bears a golden name
   Unto the grave;
And when unto thy wedded lord
   Thou provest untrue,
Then let my bitter curses still
   Thy soul pursue:
Then with a smiling chear go thou,
As right and reason doth allow;
   Yet shew the king thou bear'st no strumpet's mind.
I go, dear father, in a trice,
And by a sleight of fine device,
   I'll cause the king confess I'm not unkind.

Here comes the lady of my life,
   The king did say.
My father bids me, sovereign lord,
   Your will obey;
And I consent, if you will grant
   One boon to me.
I grant it thee, my lady fair,
   Whatc'er it be.

My husband is alive you know;
First let me kill him e'er I go,
    And I at your command will ever be.
Thy husband now in France doth rest.
No, no; he lies within my breast,
    And being so nigh, he will my falsehood see.

With that she started from the king,
    And took her knife,
And desperately she thought to rid
    Herself of life :
The king he started from the chair,
    Her hand to stay :
O ! noble king, you have broke your word
    With me this day.
Thou shalt not do this deed, quoth he.
Then never will I lie with thee.
    No ! then live still, and let me bear the blame ;
Live in honour and high estate
With thy true lord and wedded mate ;
    I never will attempt this suit again !

v.

## THE SPANISH LADY'S LOVE TO AN
## ENGLISH MAN.

WILL you hear a Spanish lady,
　How she woo'd an English man?
Garments gay, as rich as may be,
　Deck'd with jewels had she on;
Of a comely countenance and grace was she;
And by birth and parentage of high degree.

As his prisoner there he kept her,
　In his hands her life did lie;
Cupid's bands did tie her faster,
　By the liking of her eye;
In his courteous company was all her joy;
To favour him in any thing she was not coy.

At the last there came commandment
　For to set the ladies free;
With their jewels still adornèd,
　None to do them injury:
Alas! then said this lady gay, full woe is me:
O! let me still sustain this kind captivity.

O! gallant captain, shew some pity
　To a lady in distress;
Leave me not within the city
　For to die in heaviness;

Thou hast set this present day my body free,
But my heart in prison strong remains with thee.

How should'st thou, fair lady, love me,
  Whom thou know'st thy country's foe?
Thy fair words make me suspect thee;
  Serpents are where flowers grow.
All the evil I think to thee, most gracious knight,
God grant unto myself the same may fully light.

Blessed be the time and season
  That you came on Spanish ground:
If you may our foes be termèd,
  Gentle foes we have you found:
With our cities, you have won our hearts each one;
Then to your country, bear away that is your own.

Rest you still, most gallant lady,
  Rest you still, and weep no more;
Of fair lovers there are plenty;
  Spain doth yield a wondrous store.
Spaniards fraught with jealousie we often find;
But English men throughout the world are counted
    kind.

Leave me not unto a Spaniard,
  You alone enjoy my heart;
I am lovely, young, and tender,
  And so love is my desert;
Still to serve thee day and night my mind is prest;
The wife of every English man is counted blest.

It would be a shame, fair lady,
 For to bear a woman hence;
English soldiers never carry
 Any such without offence.
I will quickly change myself, if it be so,
And like a page I'll follow thee where'er thou go.

I have neither gold nor silver
 To maintain thee in this case;
And to travel, 'tis great charges,
 As you know, in every place.
My chains and jewels every one shall be thine own;
And eke ten thousand pounds in gold, that lies
  unknown.

On the seas are many dangers,
 Many storms do there arise,
Which will be to ladies dreadful,
 And force tears from wat'ry eyes.
Well, in worth, I could endure extremity;
For I could find in heart to lose my life for thee.

Courteous lady, be contented;
 Here comes all that breeds the strife;
I, in England, have already
 A sweet woman to my wife:
I will not falsifie my vow for gold or gain,
Nor yet for all the fairest dames that live in Spain.

Oh! how happy is that woman
 That enjoys so true a friend;

Many days of joy God send you!
  Of my suit I'll make an end:
Upon my knees I pardon crave for this offence,
Which love and true affection did first commence.


Commend me to thy loving lady;
  Bear to her this chain of gold,
And these bracelets for a token;
  Grieving that I was so bold:
All my jewels, in like sort, bear thou with thee;
For these are fitting for thy wife, and not for me:


I will spend my days in prayer,
  Love and all her laws defie;
In a nunnery will I shroud me,
  Far from other company;
But ere my prayers have end, be sure of this,
For thee and for thy love I will not miss.


Thus farewel! most gentle captain,
  And farewel my heart's content;
Count not Spanish ladies wanton,
  Though to thee my love was bent.
Joy and true prosperity go still with thee;
The like fall ever to thy share, most fair lady.

VI.

## A FAREWEL TO LOVE.

Farewel, false love, the oracle of lies,
  A mortal foe, an enemy to rest;
An envious boy, from whence great cares arise,
  A bastard vile, a beast with rage possest;
A way for error, a tempest full of treason,
In all respect contràry unto reason.

A poison'd serpent cover'd all with flowers;
  Mother of sighs, and murtherer of repose;
A sea of sorrows, whence run all such showers
  As moisture gives to every grief that grows;
A school of guile, a nest of deep deceit;
A golden hook that holds a poison'd bait:

A fortress fled, which reason did defend;
  A syren's song, a servage of the mind;
A maze wherein afflictions find no end;
  A raging cloud that runs before the wind;
A substance like the shadow of the sun;
A goal of grief for which the wisest run:

A quenchless fire, a nurse of trembling fear;
  A path that leads to peril and mishap;
A true retreat of sorrow and despair;
  An idle boy that sleeps in pleasure's lap;
A deep mistrust of that which certain seems;
A hope of that which reason doubtful deems.

K

Then since thy reign my younger years betray'd,
   And for my faith ingratitude I find,
And such repentance hath the wrong bewray'd,
   Whose crooked course hath not been over kind,
False love go back, and beauty frail, adieu,
Dead is the root from which such fancies grew.

---

### VII.

### THE LOVER BY HIS GIFTS THINKING TO CONQUER CHASTITY.

The lover by his gifts thinks to conquer chastity ;
And with his gifts sends these verses to his lady.

WHAT face so fair that is not carkt with gold?
   What wit so worthy has not in gold its wonder?
What learning but with golden lines doth hold?
   What state so high, but gold could bring it under?
What thought so sweet but gold doth better season?
And what rule better than the golden reason?

The ground is fat that yields the golden fruit,
   The study high that sets the golden state ;
The labour sweet that gets the golden suit,
   The reckoning rich that scorns the golden rate ;
The love is sure that golden hope doth hold,
And rich again that serves the god of gold.

---

VIII.

## THE WOMAN'S ANSWER.

FOUL is the face whose beauty gold can grace,
　Worthless the wit that hath gold in her wonder;
Unlearned lines put gold in honour's place,
　Wicked the state that will to coin come under;
Bad the conceit that season'd is with gold,
And beggar's rule that such a reason hold.

Earth gives the gold, but heaven gives greater grace;
　Men study wealth, but angels wisdom praise:
Labour seeks peace, love hath an higher place,
　Death makes the reck'ning, life is all my race;
Thy hope is here; my hope of heaven doth hold;
God give me grace, let Dives die with gold.

FINIS.

# NOTES.

*Editions of the Garland of Good-Will.* Dr. Rimbault has favoured the editor with the following account of posthumous editions of the Garland : the information was received too late for the Preface.

*An edition dated* 1631. This is in black letter, and is in the Bodleian Library. [Said to be printed by Eliz. Allde.]

*Edition dated* 1659. Black letter. Printed for J. Wright. A copy, supposed to be unique, is in the possession of J. A. Repton, Esq., of Springfield House, Chelmsford.

*Edition dated* 1678. Black letter. [This is fully described in our preface ; and being by the same publisher as the one of 1659, it is probably a reprint. The design on the title-page is also found in the title-page of Deloney's *Thomas of Reading.* 1632.]

*Edition of* 1685. Printed by J. Millett. A copy was sold at Heber's sale, and afterwards appeared in Thorpe's Catalogue, 1836. No other copy is known, nor can it be ascertained who is the present possessor.

*Edition of* 1688. A copy is *believed* to be in the Pepysian Library. [This edition is probably one of Wright's.]

*Edition of* 1696. No information can be obtained respecting it. [Is it not identical with the next-named edition ?]

*Edition of* 1709. Printed for G. Conyers. [This is described in our preface. It is without date, and the Editor of the present edition agrees with Dr. Rimbault in believing it to be of no earlier date than 1709 ; but as 1696 has been assigned as its *real* date, may it not be the same as that described as of 1696, *supra ?*] No particulars can be obtained of any editions published in the author's lifetime, nor of any editions printed subsequently to that of Conyers.

Page 10, l. 1. *The flower-de-leuce in Cheapside.* The house of Jane Shore was in Ludgate, in or near Flower-de-luce court, which no longer exists, its site being now occupied by the London Coffee House. She was, according to a letter of Richard III, which is preserved in the Harleian MSS. the wife of William Shore, a goldsmith : the Fleur-de-lis, to speak heraldically, was always represented as *Argent* or *Or*, and was, therefore, a fitting sign to designate the calling of her husband.

Page 12. *A song of king Edgar.* Mason's lyric drama of Elfrida is founded on this ballad, as are also two very heavy dramatic affairs by Aaron Hill. It would appear from the following extract that Deloney's ballad is founded on a passage in William of Malmsbury's Chronicle.

"There was," says the historian, " in his [Edgar's] time, one Athelwold, a nobleman of great celebrity, and one of his confidants. The king had commissioned him to visit Elfthrida, daughter of Ordgar, duke [chieftain] of Devonshire, (whose charms had so fascinated the eyes of some persons, that they commended her to the king) and to offer her marriage, if her beauty were really equal to report. Hastening on his embassy, and finding every thing consonant to general estimation, he concealed his mission from her parents, and procured the damsel for himself. Returning to the king, he told a tale which made for his own purpose, that she was a girl nothing out of the common track of beauty, and by no means worthy of such transcendant dignity. When Edgar's heart was disengaged from this affair, and employed on other amours, some tattlers acquainted him how completely Athelwold had duped him by his artifices. Paying him in his own coin, that is, returning him deceit for deceit, he showed the earl a fair countenance, and, as in a sportive manner, appointed a day when he would visit his far-famed lady. Terrified almost to death with this dreadful pleasantry, he hastened before to his wife, entreating that she would administer to his safety by attiring herself as unbecomingly as possible ; then first disclosing the intention of such a proceeding. But what did not this woman dare ? She was hardy enough to deceive the confidence of her first lover, her first husband, to call up every charm by art, and to omit nothing which would stimulate the desire of a young and powerful man. Nor did events happen contrary to her design. For he fell so desperately in love with her the moment he saw her, that, dissembling his indignation, he sent for the earl into a wood at Wharewelle [Whorwell, Hants] called Harewood, under pretence of hunting, and ran him through with a javelin ; and when the illegitimate son of the murdered nobleman approached with his accustomed familiarity, and was asked by the king how he liked that kind of sport, he is reported to have said, ' Well, my sovereign liege, I ought not to be displeased with that which gives you pleasure.' This answer so assuaged the mind of the raging monarch, that, for the remainder of his life, he held no one in greater estimation than this young man; mitigating the offence of this tyrannical deed against the father by royal solicitude for the son. In expiation of this crime, a monastery, which was built on this spot by Elfthrida, is inhabited by a large congregation of nuns." See Dr.

Giles's translation of *Malmsbury's Chronicle.* Bohn's Edition. London, 1847 ; pp. 159-60.

Page 18. *How Coventry was made free, &c.* This popular legend does not seem to have the slightest historical foundation. William of Malmsbury, and other church historians, relate the munificent gifts of Leofric and his wife Godifa, such as their founding monasteries at Coventry and elsewhere, but are wholly silent on the subject of the lady's equestrian performance *in puris naturalibus.*

Page 21. *The duke of Cornwal's daughter.* This tale appears to be taken from the chronicle of Geoffrey of Monmouth. See Bohn's Edition. London, 1848, p. 109.

Page 30. *The banishment of the two dukes of Hereford and Norfolk.* This story is related by several of the old chroniclers, who are not agreed as to the catastrophe.

Page 36, l. 17. *Hoised* sail. The phrase is found in Shakespeare and Ben Johnson, and in several other writers of the Elizabethan era. Evans, from sheer ignorance, see his *Old Ballads,* has altered the word "hoised" to *hoisted!* The commonest school dictionary, if he had consulted it, would have taught him better.

Page 38. *The noble acts of Arthur, &c.* It will be seen from the following extract, that this ballad is a poetical and tolerably literal version of portions of three chapters in *La Mort D'Arthur,* by Sir Thos. Malory, Knt., (1485.)

"And so Sir Launcelot departed, and, by adventure, came into the same forest whereas he was taken sleeping. And in the midst of an highway he met with a damsel riding upon a white palfrey, and either saluted other. 'Fair damsel,' said Sir Launcelot, 'know ye in this country any adventures ?' 'Sir knight,' said the damsel to Sir Launcelot, 'here are adventures near hand, an thou durst prove them ?' 'Why should I not prove adventures ?' said Sir Launcelot, 'as for that cause came I hither.' 'Well,' said the damsel, 'thou seemest well to be a right good knight, and if thou dare meet with a good knight, I shall bring thee whereas the best knight is, and the mightiest that ever thou found ; so that thou wilt tell me what thy name is, and of what country and knight thou art.' 'Damsel, as for to tell thee my name, I take no great force : truly, my name is Sir Launcelot du Lake !' 'Sir, thou beseemest well ; here be adventures that be fallen for thee ; for hereby dwelleth a knight that will not be over-matched for no man that I know, but ye over match him. And his name is Sir Turquine ; and, as I understood, he hath in his prison, of king Arthur's court, good knights three score and four that he hath won with his own hands. But when ye have done this tournay, ye shall promise me, as ye are a true knight, for to go with me, and help me and other damsels that are distressed with a false knight.' 'All your intent and desire, damsel, I will fulfil, so that ye will bring me to this knight.' 'Now, fair knight, come on your way !' And so she brought him unto the ford, and unto the tree whereon the bason hung. So Sir Launcelot let his horse drink ; and after, he beat on the bason with the end of his spear so hard, and with such a might, that he made the bottom fall out, and long he did so, but he saw nothing. Then he rode endlong the gates of the manor well nigh half an hour. And then was he ware of a great knight that drove an horse afore him, and overthwart the horse lay an armed knight bound. And ever, as they came nearer and nearer, Sir Launcelot thought he should know him ; then Sir Launcelot was ware that it was Sir Gaheris, Sir Gawaine's brother, a knight of the *Table Round.* ' Now, fair damsel,' said Sir Launcelot, ' I see yonder comes a knight fast bound, which is a fellow of mine, and brother he is unto Sir Gawaine ; and at the first beginning I promise you, by the leave of God, to rescue that knight ; but if his master set the better in the saddle, I shall deliver all the prisoners out of danger ; for I am sure that he hath two brethren of mine prisoners with him.' By that time that either had seen other, they took their spears unto them. ' Now, fair knight,' said Sir Launcelot, ' put that wounded knight from thy horse, and let him rest awhile, and then let us two prove our strength together. For as it is informed and shewed me, thou doest, and hast done great despite and shame unto the knights of the *Round Table,* and, therefore, defend thee now shortly.' 'An thou be of the *Round Table,*' said Sir Turquine, ' I defy thee and all thy fellow-ship ?' ' That is over much,' said Sir Launcelot.

" And then they put their spears in their rests, and came together with their horses as fast as it was possible for them to run, and either smote other in the midst of their shields, that both their horses' backs burst under them ; whereof the knights were both astonied ; and as soon as they might avoid their horses, they took their shields afore them, and drew out their swords, and came together eagerly ; and either gave other many strokes, for there might neither shields nor harness hold their dints. And so within awhile they had both grimly wounds, and bled passing grievously. Thus they fared two hours or more trasing, and rasing, either other where they might hit any bare place. At the last they were both breathless, and stood leaning on their swords. ' Now fellow,' said Sir Turquine, ' hold thy hand

awhile, and tell me what I shall ask thee.' 'Say on,' said
Sir Launcelot. 'Thou art,' said Sir Turquine, 'the biggest
man that ever I met withal, and the best breathed; and
like one knight that I hate above all other knights, and
that thou be not he, I will lightly accord with thee; and
for thy love I will deliver all thy prisoners that I have, that
is three score and four, so that thou wilt tell me thy name,
and thou and I we will be fellows together, and never fail
thee while I live.' 'It is well said,' quoth Sir Launcelot,
'but sithence it is so that I may have thy friendship, what
knight is he that thou hatest above all other?' 'Truly,'
said Sir Turquine, 'his name is Launcelot du Lake; for
he slew my brother, Sir Carados, at the dolorous tower,
which was one of the best knights then living, and, therefore,
I him except of all knights; for an I may once meet with
him, that one of us shall make an end of other, and to that
I make a vow. And for Sir Launcelot's sake I have slain
an hundred good knights, and as many I have utterly
maimed, that never after they might help themselves, and
many have died in my prison, and yet I have three score
and four, and all shall be delivered so that thou wilt tell me
thy name, and so it be that thou be not Sir Launcelot.'
'Now see I well,' said Sir Launcelot, 'that such a man I
might be, I might have peace; and such a man I might
be, there should be between us two mortal war; and now,
Sir knight, at thy request, I will that thou wit and know
that I am Sir Launcelot du Lake, king Ban's son of
Benwicke, and knight of the *Round Table*. And now I
defy thee, do thy best.' 'Ah!' said Sir Turquine, 'Launcelot,
thou art unto me most welcome as ever was any knight, for
we shall never depart till the one of us be dead.' And
then hurtled they together as two wild bulls, rushing and
lashing with their shields and swords, that sometimes they

·fell both on their noses. Thus they fought still two hours and more, and never would rest, and Sir Turquine gave Sir Launcelot many wounds, that all the ground, there as they fought, was all besprinkled with blood. Then, at the last, Sir Turquine waxed very faint, and gave somewhat back, and bare his shield full low for weariness. That soon espied Sir Launcelot, and then lept upon him fiercely as a lion, and got him by the banner of his helmet, and so he plucked him down on his knees, and, anon, rased of his helm, and then he smote his neck asunder."—*La Morte D'Arthur*. Part 1, cap. 108-9-10 ; Edit. London, 1816, pp. 227-31.

Page 71. *The Sinner's Redemption.* In a copy of this popular carol in the Roxburgh collection, it is said to be "To the tune of My Bleeding Heart, or, In Creet". The carol is ancient, but much more modern than the time of Deloney. The Editor of the present work has been favoured with a communication from W. Sandys, Esq., F.S.A., (the compiler of the best collection of carols extant), from which the following is an extract :—"The carol, 'All you that are to mirth inclined', is rather a favourite, and has been, I expect, regularly printed at the Christmas anniversary for many years back. I got two copies, with a great many other MS. carols, from an harmonious (but I fear bibulous) blacksmith in the west of Cornwall some five-and-twenty years since. Davies Gilbert, F.R.S., published a copy in his small collection. I have, I believe, three copies by Bloomer of Birmingham, (with variations) and broadside copies by Pitts, Thomson, and Batchelar of London. The copy printed in my *Carols*, p. 84, is shorter than these (except Gilbert's) by several verses ; as I adopted the shortest copy I got from Rowe the blacksmith. My copy also differs somewhat from that in *The Garland*, where it is

called the Sinner's Redemption, which name is retained to
the present time." Mr. Sandys, in the same communica-
tion, observes, "I looked into Deloney's book previous to
printing, but I could not meet with a black-letter copy".
This carol is also to be found in a small, but very good col-
lection of carols, without date, but printed at Bilston, and
entitled, " A new Carol Book for Christmas".

Page 76. *A wonderful Prophesie, &c.* A broadside copy
of this production is preserved in the Roxburgh collection.
It bears the imprint of John White of Newcastle-on-Tyne,
and is therefore no older than the close of the last century ;
it may be a transcript of the original, but whether so or not,
it contains the following verification of the story ! "The
names of the masters of the parish who saw the maid on
her death-bed, and heard the words of the prophecy which
she declared, were as followeth : W. Wates, curate, T.
Davies, head constable, R. Wilkins, and C. Jenner, church-
wardens, who, by consent of divers others in the same
parish, which were in the presence at the damsel's decease,
caused a letter to be written, and sent it from thence to
London on purpose to have it printed ; thereby to avoid
scandal. Contrived in metre by L. P." These initials (if
correct) enable us to ascertain the author and the date of
the composition, for L. P. were the initials used by Lawrence
Price, a popular ballad-writer, who flourished between 1642
and 1673. He wrote many chap-books, and one which still
retains its fame, viz., *The famous History of Valentine and
Orson.* The Rev. Richard Tyacke, the present clergyman
of Padstow, says, " There is no tradition whatever existing
in this place in regard to the legend of the maid of Pad-
stow ; but *James* is a parochial name : Jenner and Wilkins
are not, and do not seem ever to have been so." We may

therefore conclude that the story is a fiction, and that the ballad is what the flying stationers term " a cock".

Page 89. *A pleasant song between Plain Truth and Blind Ignorance.*  Percy calls the language put into the mouth of " Ignorance" the Somersetshire dialect, and supposes the scene to be Glastonbury Abbey ; but the so-presumed Somerset dialect is nothing more than the *patois* which all our old dramatists are in the habit of putting into the mouths of their countrymen, and to localize which would be about as easy a task as an attempt to localize the strange jargon used by the countrymen of our modern playwrights.  By *learned doctor*, see page 94, l. 8, is evidently meant Dr. Martin Luther.  In the last verse of the song, Percy has improved the *theology* by conjectural emendation. The present Editor, however, has stuck to the text, bearing in mind that the speaker is " Ignorance", who, though styled by some the parent of devotion, is certainly not a very orthodox commentator.

Page 103. *A princely ditty, &c.*  This song is evidently in honour of queen Elizabeth, though said " to be translated from the French".  It may probably be of French origin, but the Editor has not been able to trace it.

Page 105. *Fancy and Desire.*  This poem is by Edward Vere, earl of Oxford ; for further information respecting the author, who flourished in the reign of Elizabeth, the reader is referred to *Percy's Reliques*, Vol. i, Book 1.

Page 107. *Crabbed Age and Youth.*  The first verse is found in Shakespeare's *Passionate Pilgrim*, and therefore the song has always been ascribed to our great bard ; but as many of the songs scattered over the plays and poems of Shakespeare are known to be the productions of his contemporaries, as Marlowe and others, the Editor must require some stronger evidence than any which has yet been adduced, to satisfy him that Deloney is not the author of Crabbed Age and Youth. As a proof that the *Passionate Pilgrim* has no claim to be considered the entire production of Shakspeare, it is only necessary to point out that it contains *Marlowe's* well-known song, " *Come live with me and be my love*". No author was more quoted by the Elizabethan dramatists than Deloney.

Page 111. *As you came from the Holy Land.* In the Bodleian Library (MS. Rawl. Poet. 85, fol. 124) is a copy of this ballad, with " W. R." appended to it, and therefore certain antiquaries have jumped to the conclusion that Sir Walter Raleigh is the author. Percy takes no notice of the claim set up for Raleigh, nor does it appear to be generally known. Dr. Bliss, in his edition of the *Athenæ Oxonienses*, ii, 248, prints the ballad from the Bodleian MS., but *he* evidently did not know of the copy in Deloney's *Garland;* and the Rev. J. Hannah, in his edition of *Poems of Wotton, Raleigh, and others*, also prints from the same MS., and ascribes the poem to Raleigh ! Surely our old minstrel poet is not to be robbed of his claim to the ballad, on such slender authority as the existence of a manuscript (written by nobody knows whom), merely because it happens to be signed " W. R."

Page 113. *The Winning of Cales.* The victory celebrated in this very spirited sea song was gained on the 21st June, 1596. In both editions of the Garland (See Preface) the burden is " Englishmen *comes*". Percy, who corrected his copy by the reading of the celebrated folio manuscript, gives the chorus as it is in the preceding pages, thinking, no doubt, that it was even better to follow a manuscript of very questionable authority, than to perpetuate a violation of grammar.

Page 125. *The Spanish lady's love.* According to some accounts, the hero of this ballad was of the family of the Pophams of Littlecot : another tradition represents one of the Levisons of Trentham as the hero ; and another legend would have us believe that the hero was one of the family of Bolte, of Thorpe Hall, Lincolnshire. The story is a very common one, and is probably the invention of the poet. The reader will find the evidence in favour of the various claimants in *Percy's Reliques,* Vol. i, Part 2, and also in Rimbault's *Musical Illustrations of Percy's Reliques* (Cramer and Co., London, 1850), a work of considerable research, and well deserving the notice of all admirers of our ancient melodies.

Page 126, l. 25. *Prest, i.e.,* ready. As in the fine old version of the 104th Psalm,

" Lightnings to serve, we see also *prest.*"

Page 129. *A Farewel to Love.* This is set to music by Wm. Byrd, and was published by him as a madrigal in 1588. Byrd's copy does not contain the last verse, and the other stanzas are given with considerable variations.

# REMARKS ON TUNES

### MENTIONED IN

## The Garland of Good-Will.

---

Page 1. *Flying Fame*. This is one of the tunes to which Chevy Chace was sung. It is reprinted in Chappell's *National English Airs*.

Page 9. *The Hunt is up*. The ballad is in a different measure to that of the song *The Hunt is up*, printed by Mr. John Payne Collier in his *Extracts from the Registers of the Stationers' Company*, and could not be sung to the same tune. It is probably the air often referred to as "Shore's Wife", but which has not been recovered.

Page 12. *Labandulishot*. This tune is *mentioned* in *A Handefull of Pleasant Delites*, 1584, and that is all we know about it. The meaning of the word "Labandulishot" is a mystery, and likely to remain so.

Page 18. *Prince Arthur died at Ludlow*. This tune cannot be traced ; although from the number of ballads directed to be sung to it, it may probably exist under some other name.

*qi idw: " in Creete·*

Page 21. *In Greece.* This is the same tune as "Queen Dido". See *Musical Illustrations to Percy's Reliques :* it is still a popular ballad tune, and in the north of England "The Bowes Tragedy", and other dolorous ditties, are chanted to it by village crones.

Page 46. *The Ghost's Hearse.* Nothing is known of this tune.

Page 49. *Robinson's Almain.* A tune composed by Thomas Robinson, Lutenist, author of *The Schoole of Musicke,* 1603, and *New Citharen Lessons,* 1609.

Page 52. *Crimson Velvet.* This tune will be found in *Friesche Lust-hof,* 1634, and is reprinted in Rimbault's *Musical Illustrations to Percy's Reliques of Ancient Poetry.*

Page 68. *Hey ho, holiday.* This tune may be found in *Pavans, Galliards, Almains, and other short Airs &c., made by Anthony Holborne,* 1599.

Page 71. *The Sinner's Redemption,* is, according to the Roxburgh copy (see p. 140 *ante*), to be sung " to the tune of My Bleeding Heart, or In Creet". Dr. Rimbault thinks that two tunes are here alluded to ; neither of them is known. The carol is *now* generally sung to a tune which is a version of the one sung to "Death and the Lady".

Page 76. *In Summer-time.* There are several tunes called by this name, but the only known one to which this ballad *could* be sung, is contained in Hall's *Courte of Vertue,* a godly antidote to *The Courte of Venus,* and printed in 1565. It is, however, very questionable whether the bar-

barous tune in Hall's book is the one alluded to at page 76. The airs contained in *The Courte of Vertue* are puzzles, even to a musical antiquary, and it is a difficult matter to decide whether they are ballad or psalm tunes ; if the latter, they certainly seem more adapted for the accompaniment of the "Pig Virginal", described in Bayle's *Dictionary*, and Avison's *Treatise on Musical Expression*, than for the organ.

Page 82. *The Bride's Good Morrow.* This tune has not been recovered.

Page 111. *As I came from Walsingham.* The tune of *Walsingham* is to be found in Queen Elizabeth's Virginal book, and is reprinted in Chappell's *National English Airs.*

Page 113. *The Winning of Cales.* Dr. Rimbault identifies this tune with *Tantara rara masks all*, by a manuscript Virginal book (temp. James I) in his possession. See *Musical Illustrations to Percy's Reliques of Ancient Poetry*, p. 23. If this tune were introduced on the stage with appropriate musical accompaniments, it could not fail of becoming popular. The following arrangement is by Joseph Hart, Jun., Esq., the author of " I'd rather be an Englishman", &c. &c.

Page 125. *The Spanish Lady.* This truly beautiful tune is contained in several of the ballad operas printed about 1798, and will be found in Chappell's *National English Airs.* The following arrangement is by Mr. Joseph Hart, Jun.

Page 129. *A farewell to Love.* See note page 144.

# The Winning of Cales.

*Moderately quick.*

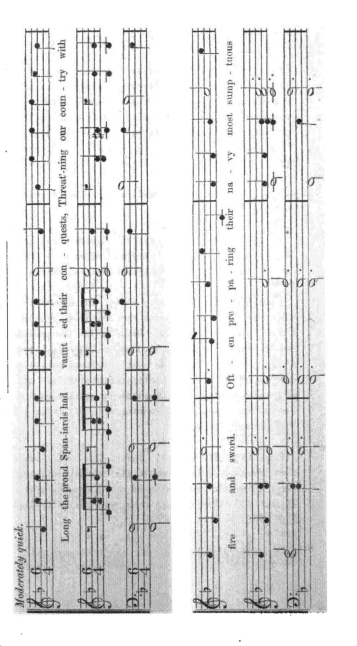

Long the proud Span-iards had vaunt - ed their con - quests, Threat'-ning our coun - try with fire and sword. Oft - en pre - pa - ring their na - vy most sump - tuous with

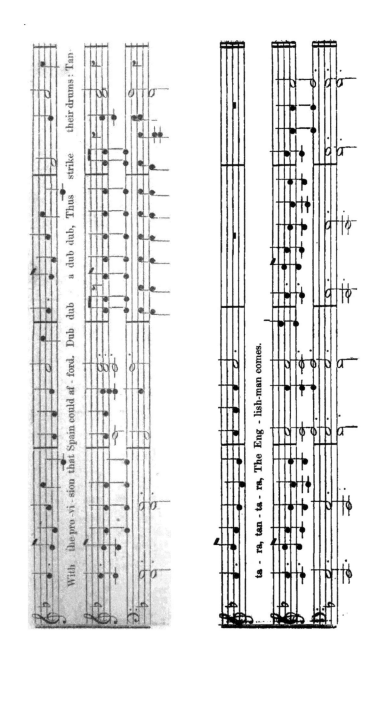

9 781010 703587